DESIGN
THINGS THAT
MAKE SENSE

DEBORAH NAS

TECH. INNOVATOR'S GUIDE

COMBINE DESIGN STRATEGIES TO STRENGTHEN BENEFITS AND MITIGATE RESISTANCE, AND YOU MIGHT STRIKE GOLD

Sensing a Need for
DESIGN STRATEGIES

N ew technologies fascinate me. They unlock possibilities and add value to our lives. I was lucky to grow up in a family that welcomed new technologies and tech products. Some of my most vivid memories include playing Pong on our TV set, using my brother's Sinclair "home computer," and taking apart a classic radio with my father to see what was inside. The technological progress that I witnessed with my own eyes made a lasting impression; those big, beautiful tubes I discovered inside the old radio seemed ancient compared to the small electronics inside the transistor radio-cassette player in our living room.

My curiosity led me to study Industrial Design Engineering at the Delft University of Technology, where I learned about new product development and innovation. After graduation, I applied my innovation skills as a corporate employee and went on to co-found a boutique innovation agency to help companies innovate more effectively. Today, I act as a sparring partner for management teams and startup founders. I also take pride in being a part-time professor at the faculty I once attended, teaching strategic design for technology-based innovation.

Technology-based innovation differs from user-centered innovation in many ways and presents its own unique challenges. First, while user-centered innovation is driven by the demand for a solution to a particular problem, technology-based innovation is often sparked by a novel technological capability. This can give birth to new-to-the-world product concepts that are difficult for people to understand. Second, the suspicion many people have of new technologies hinders the testing of new product concepts. Finally, innovation teams consist mostly of engineers untrained in innovation and design. As a result, the technological capabilities of new products usually take precedent over the people they're intended to serve, leading to products that haven't been considered from a user's perspective. This limits commercial success and can even cause commercial failure. For technology-based innovation to be successful, the entire process must be infused with people-focused thinking.

Theory about technology adoption and generic innovation processes is plentiful. However, not much has been written about technology-based innovation in light of designing successful consumer products, i.e., products that people adopt and love using. When I work with innovation teams to help ensure their products will be successful, I am very hands-on. It wasn't until I began teaching at university that I realized how difficult it is to quickly teach people technology-based innovation and equip them with the same knowledge and skills that I was applying in my work life every day. Therefore, I made it my mission to create a practical knowledge source for everybody working in technology-based innovation.

The foundations of successful innovation are great ideas and excellent execution. Although this book may inspire you to come up with great ideas, it is mostly intended to help you develop great ideas into successful products.

In preparation for this book, I researched many technology, psychology, innovation, and design theories. I analyzed countless products, drew inspiration from discussions with peers, and built on 25 years of hands-on experience. I ideated, prototyped, and involved many experts along the way. The result of my research and design journey is a set of design strategies that can help you create tech products whose technological benefits far outweigh their potential drawbacks.

I created this book, the "Tech Innovator's Guide," for all innovators who apply new technologies in their products. Working with innovators in the field has taught me that it's easy to recognize products that make sense but challenging to create them. Engineers, innovation managers, product managers, product owners, developers, startup founders, and any other innovators with or without industrial design training can all make use of this guide.

The design strategies can help you identify opportunities at the start of your innovation process, act as an inspirational tool in brainstorming sessions, and help you recognize improvement points for existing products.

These design strategies will also help you and your team infuse people-focused thinking into your innovation process. They will help you to design Things That Make Sense.

Now, go innovate!
Deborah Nas

I made it my mission to create a practical knowledge source for everybody working in technology-based innovation

THE DESIGN STRATEGIES IN THIS BOOK
ATTENTION
ARE EXTREMELY POWERFUL

USE YOUR POWER FOR GOOD

While technological innovation advanced society and brought humankind extraordinary benefits, it can be a double-edged sword. The cars brought to us by oil and the combustion engine offered freedom of movement, but also polluted our air. The transistor gave birth to electronics, but has also led to the rapid depletion of scarce resources and massive amounts of electronic waste. The internet and algorithms have added a digital dimension to our lives that unleashed valuable freedoms and functionality, but also gave birth to powerful big tech companies and sophisticated surveillance.

Technological innovation is driven by technology optimists; people who instinctively focus on the positives of new technologies. In the early stages of technology development, the negatives of a new technology are much more difficult to envision, as it is often unknown how exactly these technologies will be applied and what type of products they will bring forth.

We, the innovators, apply these new technologies and use them to create new products. As such, we bear a major role in shaping our world. Our actions and the products we create will inevitably have consequences, whether intended or unintended. We should therefore hold ourselves to an ethical and moral standpoint when developing new products, thinking things through carefully at every stage, from when we first launch a product all the way up until the moment it becomes a commodity.

Moral application of technology is becoming increasingly important as next-generation AI, quantum computing, genomics, VR, blockchain, and the rest of tomorrow's technologies are expected to impact society in profound ways, unmatched by any past progress. It is our job, as innovators, to make sense of it all—to see the hidden opportunities at the intersection of what is right for people, business, and the world.

Here, I share with you the Tech Innovator's Oath that I adhere to. I invite you to consider your own moral and ethical stance as an innovator and add elements as you see fit.

Visit www.designthingsthatmakesense.com to make additions, sign the oath, and share it with others.

The Tech Innovator's Oath:

**I COMMIT TO DESIGNING
TECH PRODUCTS THAT MAKE SENSE
TO ALL STAKEHOLDERS INVOLVED.
IN DOING SO, I WILL:**

- Take responsibility for my creations and be accountable for their effects
- Be open to feedback and criticism, especially from technology critics
- Critically assess whether or not technology is the best way to address the challenge at hand
- Never pursue business goals at the expense of people, society, or our planet
- Create, build on, and make use of open source technology as much as possible
- Do everything in my power to prevent unintended consequences from scaling my product
- Strive to create a positive impact
- Speak up if others are acting contrary to this tech oath
- Type here |

CONTENTS

TECHNOLOGY-BASED INNOVATION

STRENGTHEN BENEFITS

MITIGATE RESISTANCE

24 DESIGN STRATEGIES
TO STRENGTHEN BENEFITS

B1	Customize	B13	Evoke Joy
B2	Personalize	B14	Shape Memories
B3	Make It Simple	B15	Stimulate Learning
B4	Save Time	B16	Provide Insight
B5	Make It Hassle-Free	B17	Fuel Motivation
B6	Enable Anytime, Anywhere	B18	Drive Social Interaction
B7	Offer Structure	B19	Deliver Prestige
B8	Guide Decision Making	B20	Boost Social Impact
B9	Save Money	B21	Facilitate Sharing
B10	Increase Efficiency	B22	Lengthen Lifespan
B11	Elevate Performance	B23	Reduce Footprint
B12	Delight the Senses	B24	Unleash New Value

13 DESIGN STRATEGIES TO MITIGATE RESISTANCE

R1   Increase Personal Safety

R2   Preserve Data Privacy

R3   Offer Transparency

R4   Make It Secure

R5   Increase Control

R6   Ensure Compatibility

R7   Be Future-Proof

R8   Comply with Regulations

R9   Build Partnerships

R10   Fit Social Norms

R11   Make It (In)visible

R12   Create Familiarity

R13   Design for Marketing Strategies

TECHNOLOGY-BASED

INNOVATION

DESIGN THINGS

As the things we design become increasingly connected and complicated, we can't view them in an isolated way. Innovations based on new technologies are often combinations of products, services, business models, infrastructure, data, or even entire ecosystems. They have become "things" that are increasingly challenging to define.

Over the last few decades, many products have evolved from stand-alone, physical items to highly connected products that live in both the physical and virtual world. Cars have evolved from mechanical machines to "AI-powered, networked, self-driving computers on wheels." On top of that, new business models have emerged. You can purchase your own car, share a car with others, buy a car subscription, or get access to a car as part of "mobility as a service." So what exactly are you paying for? A product? A service? A product-service system? A shared infrastructure? A concept?

For the sake of readability, I will refer to these difficult-to-define things as "products," as is common in the tech scene. "Product" can denote a pair of high-tech headphones, a voice-controlled virtual assistant that supports your life in many ways, a connected coffee machine that automatically orders coffee when you run out, a blockchain-enabled smart mortgage, a self-driving shared car, or anything else that makes use of new technologies.

Today, examples of such new technologies are artificial intelligence (AI), virtual reality (VR), augmented reality (AR), blockchain, robotics, 3D printing, etc. Soon, nano or quantum technologies may make the list. Who knows what the future might bring?

THAT MAKE SENSE

A product that makes sense is a critical success factor for any business. Of course, there are many other factors involved like the right team, good timing, adequate funding, great marketing, and widespread distribution. In practice, I see many innovators blaming these factors when success doesn't come about, while a trained eye can discern that flaws in the product's design are actually the underlying cause of failure. Products are often hard to understand, expensive, raise (privacy) concerns, or are simply lacking the right set of features.

PRODUCTS THAT MAKE SENSE TO CONSUMERS:

- Are easy to understand and easy to explain to others.

- Create value by fulfilling consumers' needs.

- Address consumers' fears and concerns over the technologies the products rely on.

PRODUCTS THAT MAKE SENSE TO THE COMPANY CREATING THEM:

- Fit the company's purpose.

- Fit the company's brand and market strategy.

- Create financial value, brand value, market reach value, or strategic value.

WHAT MAKES SENSE TO YOU AS AN INNOVATOR*?

- . . .

- . . .

- . . .

*It's up to you to decide what makes sense to you.

For me, products make sense if they fit into my ethical framework (see the Tech Oath) and unlock new value for users or deliver known value in a superior way. In addition, every element must form one logical whole when combined. When I see a product that makes sense, there's an immediate flash of recognition that the product has those crucial qualities I'm always on the lookout for, and my innovator's heartbeat quickens.

Making Sense of Technology
ADOPTION AND RESISTANCE

Not everyone is equally open to new technologies. Some people are first in line to try out new things, while others wait until it's proven to work or never embrace it at all. Some people even actively oppose technological innovations. Throughout history, new technologies have always triggered suspicion and fear, with AI being today's most prominent example. This resistance against technological innovation should not be ignored, as it often sheds light on how innovations may negatively affect society. We should understand resistance in order to design better products: products that maximize value and minimize harm.

Our inclination towards using new technologies is determined by four different qualities that measure our individual technology readiness. The first two, optimism and innovativeness, are motivators; they make people likely to adopt new technologies. Optimism is a positive view of technology. It is the belief that technology offers people increased control, flexibility, and efficiency in their lives. Innovativeness is the tendency to be a technology pioneer and thought leader. The other two qualities, discomfort and insecurity, are inhibitors that delay or prevent technology adoption. Discomfort is a perceived lack of control over technology or the sensation of being overwhelmed by it. Insecurity is a distrust of technology, stemming from skepticism about its ability to work properly and concerns about its potentially harmful consequences[1].

People that quickly adopt technological innovations have high technology readiness levels. As Rogers famously framed it, adoption starts with innovators (2.5%), followed by early adopters (13.5%), then the early majority (34%), the late majority (34%), and finally laggards (16%)[2]. His model describes the people who, after evaluating a product, decide to adopt (get it now) or postpone (get it later), adding up to 100% of adopters. However, it doesn't consider people who reject (never get) or oppose (actively fight) products. In reality, the likelihood that an innovation reaches 100% adoption is nearly zero.

Besides focusing on product benefits, we must address people's fears and concerns regarding new technologies in our product designs. This can increase our chances of success by helping us reach the early majority, an indicator that an innovation might "take off." It might also boost overall adoption rates.

The smartphone is one of few examples of an innovation with an incredible speed of adoption and unusually high adoption rates. Ten years after the first iPhone launch, adoption rates of smartphones in the US and individual European countries vary between 70-90%[3]; the curve has now almost flattened. Some consumer groups have even begun moving in the opposite direction. People exchange their smartphones for regular mobile phones because they feel their privacy rights are being violated and their autonomy is shrinking. Although once adopters, these people have now become rejectors and opposers.

Resistance against technological innovation in itself is ageless, but the technologies we resist change over time. For example, people were once certain that proximity to an electrical outlet was enough to give them a shock. Cars in the UK were forbidden to drive faster than 5 km per hour to protect pedestrians. People thought the telephone would attract evil spirits and that movies would lead to the disintegration of morality.

As our lifestyles become reliant on the technologies we once feared, we tend to laugh at those fears. We cannot imagine a life without electricity; we rely on cars for our mobility, we are glued to our smartphones, and we trust modern-day "movies" on Netflix and YouTube to relax and inform us. The technologies we grew up with and are accustomed to have become integral parts of our lives. While we tend to trust the technologies we grew up with, we often fear new technologies.

Fears today include humans playing god by genetically modifying other humans, big tech companies controlling our lives, democratic countries turning into high-tech surveillance states, and AI-powered robots overtaking humanity.

Resistance to new technology can also play out on a much smaller scale. When consumers decide to adopt or reject a tech product they weigh the benefits of the product against its potential drawbacks. For example, new parents feel a strong need to care for their children and keep them safe. A key benefit of an internet-connected baby video monitor is the ability to stay in touch with their baby from anywhere. While the monitors offer clear value, parents who are afraid of hackers spying on their child might not buy one.

On the other hand, if the benefits are too weak, mitigating resistance by making your baby monitor extra secure won't make parents buy the product. Other baby monitors might offer stronger benefits, like better resolutions, a battery for mobile use, customized lullabies, or the automatic creation of movie clips that show the "highlights" of the night. Offering strong benefits is imperative.

While we tend to trust the technologies we grew up with, we often fear new technologies

Benefits are what move people forward; resistance is what holds them back. You must address both. Therefore, this book contains two distinct sections: Strengthen Benefits and Mitigate Resistance.

All too often, I've witnessed innovators disregard consumer resistance. Either they don't fully understand how consumers feel, or they believe consumers are incorrect. This ignorance breeds products that do not address potential resistance and limits commercial success. To design products that instantly make sense to consumers, we should learn from consumers' ideas, feelings, opinions, and expectations of products' benefits and drawbacks, regardless of their validity. We should want to meet consumers' needs, outperform their expectations, and address (potential) resistance throughout the design process.

You will find this book's design strategies a valuable resource for this kind of design process; they offer you a complete overview of options to strengthen benefits and mitigate resistance. They will help you to "Design Things That Make Sense."

Benefits are what move people forward; resistance is what holds them back. You must address both

❝ I've come up with a set of rules that describe our reactions to technologies.

Anything that is in the world when you're born is normal and ordinary and is just a natural part of the way the world works.

Anything that's invented between when you're fifteen and thirty-five is new and exciting and revolutionary and you can probably get a career in it.

Anything invented after you're thirty-five is against the natural order of things[4].**❞**

Douglas Adams

Technology-Based Innovation and
CONSUMER-FOCUSED THINKING

New technological capabilities are often our starting point in technology-based innovation projects. Nevertheless, our focus should be just as much on the people who will be using our products as the technologies that help create those products. We must continuously switch perspectives during the innovation process, considering it from a technology capability point of view and from a consumer point of view. After all, we can only design things that make sense to consumers if we understand their behavior, needs, and expectations. This is an area where tech innovators can significantly improve.

CB Insights' post-mortem research on tech startups reveals that five out of the top ten reasons these startups fail are directly related to not meeting customer needs[5]. They found that, on average, 70% of tech startups fail or can barely sustain themselves. The worst scores belong to consumer hardware startups, of which 97% ultimately die or become "zombies."

Although data on corporate innovation success rates is limited, my personal experience confirms a similar innovation landscape at large companies. New tech product success rates are shockingly low. Unlike startups, large corporations don't die from a failed innovation; their profitability just takes a hit. For startups, which usually begin as single-product companies, product success is a prerequisite for having a future. Their key focus should be on understanding consumer needs, as

this is critical to innovation success. However, in technology-based innovation, stepping into the consumer's shoes doesn't come easily.

Involving Consumers and Discovering Their Needs Can Be Challenging

Depending on the field of research, human needs have been defined in various different ways. For innovators, I find research from the Delft University of Technology highly useful. It defines 13 fundamental psychological needs for user-centered design practice and research[6]. See page 32 for an overview.

While understanding fundamental psychological needs is a great starting point, it is insufficient for successful innovation. You will need to understand consumer needs on a more applied level, such as needs relevant to your future product. You will find that consumers' needs are influenced by the specific circumstances that they find themselves in and by what they aspire to achieve in these circumstances. For example, people intending to use headphones while commuting or cycling in heavy traffic might have different needs and expectations than people who want to use them for concentrated work in a noisy office. While noise-canceling headphones improve the audio experience for both, they create dangerous situations for commuters, while effectively protecting office workers from their noisy environment.

For well-known products like headphones, consumer needs are relatively easy to discover. For new-to-the-world products, this is more challenging. Consumers might struggle to verbally express their needs, desires, and wishes or might not even be aware of them. This also hinders the testing of highly innovative product concepts. If consumers are not fully aware of their needs, they can have difficulty envisioning your concept's value and wonder: What problem is it solving? Why is it relevant? It takes a team of skilled innovators to uncover consumers' latent needs and connect them with technological possibilities.

Collecting consumer feedback on technological novelties might also be hindered by people's resistance to new technologies. While nobody fears a chair, many consumers fear voice-controlled digital assistants. The digital components of tech products often raise concerns. How do they work? Are the algorithms fair? What happens to my data? Recent scandals fuel our fear and suspicion of tech products and the companies that create them. This makes it challenging to test new product concepts early on in the innovation process when many details are still unclear.

Agile Innovation Methods Are Great but Need a Twist

Inspired by innovation methodologies used in software development and tech startups, most companies are adopting "agile innovation philosophies." Teams work in short cycles called "sprints" and continuously reassess and adapt plans. As new decisions regarding the product's design can be made every few weeks, teams can adjust according to market changes, technology developments, and consumer feedback. The upside of this method is significant, offering savings and flexibility.

Agile innovation also has its downsides. I see many agile innovation teams lacking well-trained innovators; teams mainly consist of computer scientists, software developers, mathematicians, and UX designers. Important decisions are made by the product owner, whose background is often business or engineering. The members all have valuable skills but often lack proper training in user-centered innovation. Many assume that inviting potential users to their sprint demo makes them user-centered, unaware that collecting feedback on a few features is not the same as an in-depth understanding of consumer needs. The reality is that many teams think "from the inside out" without realizing it. In addition, many agile teams adopt the popular belief that consumers "don't know what they want," a result of the fact that consumers can have difficulty expressing their needs. Thus, teams don't perform consumer research. They start building things as soon as possible and then measure how people respond in real life. If the product fails to gain traction, they adjust their product and try again. The result is many fatally flawed products that don't make sense to consumers and fail.

Turning the Wheels of Technology-based Innovation

Technology-based innovation is not a straightforward step-by-step process. It's a complex interplay of many different elements that ultimately make a product successful. This book aims to provide insight into all elements directly related to consumers' needs, expectations, and technology resistance.

As we've seen, technology-focused thinking often takes precedence over consumer-focused thinking in technology-based innovation. As a result, many teams simply develop a product they think is "right," often falsely assuming that their personal preferences coincide with those of consumers or assuming that novelty by itself adds sufficient value.

I'm not saying that technology-focused thinking is wrong; I'm arguing that we need to balance it with consumer-focused thinking. Ultimately, technology-focused thinking and consumer-focused thinking are equally important.

Both technological capabilities and consumer needs can be the starting point for your innovation process. However, regardless of your starting point, you need to adopt the other perspective as soon as possible.

As decisions from one perspective directly influence the other, you need to adopt an iterative approach to arrive at a product that makes sense. In the following chapters, we'll look at specific challenges for two types of innovation projects: developing new-to-the-world products and better versions of existing products.

Technology-based innovation is a complex interplay of many different elements

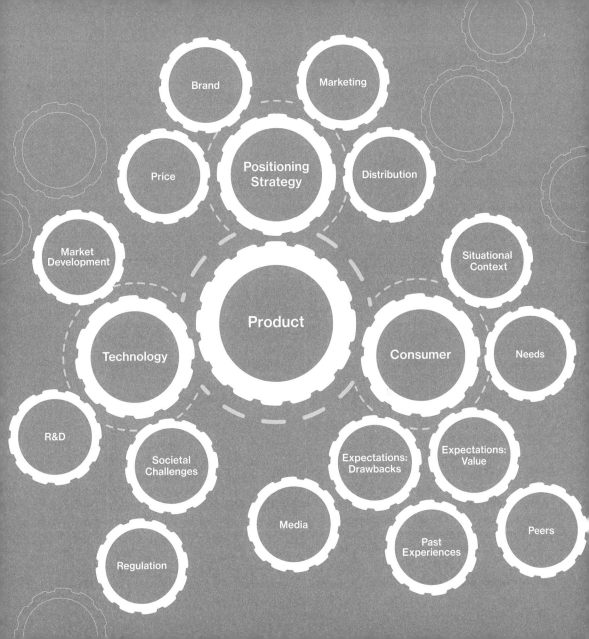

Developing
NEW-TO-THE-WORLD PRODUCTS

New-to-the-world products are typically sparked by new technologies. They are capable of things that consumers never thought possible or relevant. When presented with these products, consumers will likely have difficulty understanding what they are or what value they bring. Adoption will be slow if consumers have difficulty understanding products, potentially leading to product rejection in mainstream markets[7].

I find that innovation projects aiming to develop new-to-the-world products are the most exciting and most challenging. Challenges described in the previous chapter aside, the strategic question of how to position your product remains. Will you attempt to create an entirely new product category, or will you link your product to an existing product category? This decision will impact your product's design. To arrive at a product that makes sense, product design should go hand in hand with positioning strategy throughout the innovation process.

To illustrate how the decision to create a new category or join an existing category can affect your product, I'll use blockchain as an example. Blockchain's secure, decentralized information recording, coupled with the concept of "blockchain tokens," has the potential to revolutionize markets and unlock new value.

As I explained earlier, this book's focus is not to spot opportunities or come up with great ideas. It's about turning great ideas into successful products. Therefore, regardless how the idea came about, our starting point for this example is an idea for a blockchain-enabled product for home buyers and investors. As existing market players are slow to adopt new technologies, and many consumers are dissatisfied with traditional financial service providers, there should be fertile ground for innovation.

Before explaining the differences between creating a new category or joining an existing category, I will first explain the example's blockchain idea. This will immediately uncover one of the problems that new-to-the-world products face: you need to make an effort to reach a general understanding of the idea. Bear with me.

Context: rising real estate prices and low interest rates have caused real estate investment demand to skyrocket. However, most people don't have sufficient excess cash to buy entire homes or apartments. Investing in real estate funds could be an option, but the lack of control over the real estate these funds invest in is a dealbreaker for many people. On the other hand, first-time homebuyers often can't afford their desired home because traditional banks won't give them an adequate mortgage.

Idea: a blockchain product that addresses both investors and home buyers. Building upon the concepts of "tokenization" and "Smart contracts" in blockchain technology, you will split a home into several parts, i.e., tokens, and facilitate smooth transactions between homebuyers and individual investors without the intervention of a notary.

How it works: your platform will automatically split a single home into multiple tokens. The home buyer acquires the majority of tokens, giving them ownership of a part of the home. They either sell the remaining tokens to family or friends or offer them to the general public via your platform. People buying these tokens profit from the real estate's future value increase and get a regular payment.

Benefits: the home buyer gets a home he couldn't otherwise afford at a reasonable price. The investors' return is far higher than that of a savings account. On top of that, their risk is minimal compared to investing in the stock market. In comparison to real estate funds, investors get more control because they determine what to invest in. Investors get more flexibility and less hassle than buying and selling real estate in the traditional way; they can buy and sell tokens via your platform whenever they like.

Every transaction is registered in and automated by the blockchain. This ensures the registration is tamperproof and offers transparency to homeowners, as well as to current and future investors.

Resistance: many consumers directly link blockchain to cryptocurrencies. Newspapers write about these as shady, unregulated markets, where techies and criminals trade highly volatile virtual currencies. They are a popular payment method on the dark web and can seemingly be invented by anybody. Furthermore, the identity of blockchain's inventor is a mystery. It also comes across as difficult to use, with special software and theft-sensitive keys that you need to protect with passwords. Stories about people losing large sums of money because they forgot their password are relatively common. Traditional banks don't offer blockchain products; typically, startups work with blockchain. What happens when they fail? All these features combined could make consumers decide against taking any unnecessary risks regarding their homeownership.

In the minds of consumers, it might be challenging to understand what your product is. It's not a mortgage, nor a loan. It seems like both buying a home and renting a home at the same time. This concept's confusing nature can raise many questions, especially if people are unfamiliar with blockchain technology. They might struggle to see the value of your product's benefits, and they might experience resistance against blockchain technology.

As you can see, the example requires an awful lot of text to explain, as is the case with most new-to-the-world products. Many questions probably remain even after reading the explanation. This example's goal isn't to go into product idea details, though. The example is given to help answer the question, "How can new-to-the-world products be positioned?" Let's explore two options.

Option 1: Link to an Existing Product Category

Consumers tend to categorize new products according to their perceived similarities. Cues indicating that a new product belongs to an existing product category can aid consumers' understanding[8].

Returning to the blockchain example, you might position the product as "the 21st-century mortgage." In this case, it would be wise to include a mortgage for the home buyer to finance his tokens, i.e., his part of the home, and define the monthly payment to investors as a percentage of the total sum. These product features are similar to those of mortgages (an existing product category) and can help frame the product as a new mortgage type.

Another possibility would be framing it as "a platform for sharing homeownership." Although real estate sharing might be new, sharing platforms are a known phenomenon. To legitimize this positioning, it makes sense to charge a monthly subscription to use the platform and charge fixed fees for the initial transaction and future token ownership changes, as is common in sharing platforms.

Option 2: Create a New Product Category

To stress the product's innovativeness, you could create and name an entirely new product category, calling it something like "HomeBlocks." Analogies can be a great way to explain a new category to consumers. You could liken the product to "a stock market for homes," explaining that home buyers convert a home into shares. As the majority shareholder, they will take good care of their home, while other shareholders profit from future increases in the value of their shares and receive regular payments, similar to dividends. To support such an analogy, it is wise to incorporate product features that fit the stock market analogy. For example, a regular payment schedule denotes a "dividend" per token. Also, UX design elements could be borrowed from online consumer trade platforms like graphs with historical and actual token prices.

As you can see, your product's positioning and marketing strategies can directly influence your product design. For this reason, I have included the design strategy Design for Marketing Strategies (R13) in the Resistance part of this book. Also, new-to-the-world products are likely to encounter significant resistance from consumers. The design strategies to mitigate resistance will prove a valuable resource in your innovation process.

NEW PRODUCT CATEGORIES

New categories arise all the time. Sometimes their origin is clear, like the Polaroid Corporation launching the instant photography often referred to as "polaroid cameras and polaroid photos." Other times, one company catapults a pre-existing category into a commercially successful one, like Fitbit did for fitness trackers. In most cases, though, the growth and definition of new categories are ambiguous and involves many parties.

The way you position and market your products and who you involve can mean the difference between success and failure. If you get it right, you can become the thought leader and "owner" of a newly created category.

When Chrysler announced plans for a line of relatively small, front-wheel-drive vans in the early 1980s, they dubbed it the "minivan" category. They prompted J.D. Power, an influential market research firm in the automotive industry, to introduce the "minivan" category label in their reviews. This illustrates the role market research firms can play in defining categories, as can market analysts. Their "naming interventions," market analyses, and manufacturer categorizations carry a lot of weight.

Legislators can also play a significant part in the creation of new categories. Around the same time the minivan category was born, the American Motors Corporation lobbied the US Congress to create a new category: sport utility vehicles (SUVs). Although SUVs had always existed, they didn't have a name and were often classified as "light trucks." As the first official SUV, the 1984 Jeep Cherokee marked the start of today's best-selling car category worldwide.

Currently, an unnamed "wearable computers" category is on the rise in industrial applications. Realwear calls them "head-mounted wearable Android-class tablet computers," a name unlikely to take off. Magic Leap tries to label the new category as "wearable spatial computers," while Google Glass tries to elevate their product name "Glass" to category level, as Polaroid once did. Before these "wearable computers" enter the consumer market, either a category name will likely be established, or the existing category of "smart wearables" will be stretched to include head-worn devices.

Developing Better Versions of
EXISTING PRODUCTS

Most innovations that make it to market are improved versions of existing products; they deliver better results, have a lower price, offer higher efficiency, or bring consumers a more enjoyable user experience. When presented with these types of new product concepts, consumers will have little difficulty understanding them. After all, headphones are, well, headphones.

Your challenge lies in turning new technologies into valuable features that stand out from the crowd. Simultaneously, you must minimize possible resistance against the technologies that bring these features to life.

In my work, I see many innovators stepping into the pitfall of "feature loading" their product, making products difficult to understand and disturbing the cost-benefit balance. This is likely to happen when you overthink from a technology perspective. The solution is to first develop a deep understanding of consumers' contexts, needs, objectives, and problems they are trying to solve.

Once you have gained this understanding, you will need to dig deeper. Understanding consumers' expectations of value and possible drawbacks is a prerequisite for designing products that make sense to them. These expectations of value and drawbacks will be informed by market standards, their own past experiences, and opinions from others.

Let's assume you're working for a headphone manufacturer and you see an opportunity for headphones for office workers. They are accustomed to wearing headphones to listen to music, make video calls, and own up-to-date laptops and smartphones; their needs are various. Many of them struggle to concentrate while working in a noisy office environment. After gaining a detailed understanding of office workers' context, needs, objectives, and problems, you need to research their expectations of value and drawbacks. For example, when an office worker evaluates a new pair of headphones, they might throw the following elements into the mix:

Market standards: for new headphones, functionalities like wireless listening, noise cancellation, and a microphone for phone calls have become the norm. If headphones lack these features, they might not meet expectations of value. High-definition audio and integration with Siri or Google assistant are still a luxury feature, indicating high-end models.

Past experiences with similar products: they will pay extra attention to inconveniences they experienced firsthand, expecting their next headset to fix these. For example, their current headset can only pair with one device at a time, making it impossible to answer an incoming phone call when listening to music on their laptop.

Past experiences with different products: their wireless computer mouse needs recharging at the most inconvenient moments, making them extra sensitive to battery life performance.

Opinions from friends and peers: one of their friends might worry that wireless technology causes health issues. As a result, they might wonder if placing a Bluetooth receiver on their skull is such a good idea.

Experiences from other users: in online reviews, some people complain about the difficulty of connecting wireless headsets to different devices. While not clearly defined, the problem is one to be aware of.

Information from media: they read magazines or visit websites dedicated to consumer electronics and learn about headphones with "best buy" and "best product" awards. These awards might influence their choice.

Because forming expectations is such an ambiguous process, many more elements may play a role. These elements are in constant flux, and, as a result, so are consumers' expectations of value and drawbacks. This means that you can't rely on past consumer research. Without a deep dive into consumers' needs and their quickly evolving expectations every time you initiate a project, you are likely to miss the innovation sweet spot.

The innovation process is not a straightforward "from needs to features" process; it's an iterative process in which you frequently switch between a consumer perspective and a technological perspective. You will find direction, opportunities, and inspiration in both perspectives.

As innovators, our job is to identify what makes sense to our target consumers and develop novel products that stand out from the crowd and make perfect sense to consumers. If you succeed, consumers will easily understand your product's value over other products, experience little resistance, and adopt your product. The design strategies in this book will help you to design such products. Products that make sense.

> The innovation process is not a straightforward "from needs to features" process; it's an iterative process in which you frequently switch between a consumer perspective

MAKING SENSE OF THIS BOOK

○ This book contains two distinct sections: Strengthen Benefits and Mitigate Resistance. Use them both to design things that make sense.

○ Design strategies and tactics are supported by real-life examples, most of which come from startups. If you're reading this book sometime after its publication, these startups may have either grown into well-known market leaders... or ceased to exist. The world of innovation is ever-changing.

○ Successful innovation is not about incorporating as many design strategies as possible; it is about making the right choices. Most successful products rely on one to three design strategies in their positioning.

○ Each design strategy contains several tactics, which are ways to make that design strategy a reality. While informed by theory, these tactics are mainly derived from numerous case studies. More tactics will be added over time; visit the website to keep up to date.

○ In most cases, benefits form the basis for a product's positioning. However, in some cases, a design strategy from Mitigate Resistance can become key to a product's positioning. For example, suppose people fear being listened to when using voice-controlled products. In that case, a secure version can set itself apart from other products by offering privacy as a key benefit.

○ Some design strategies are difficult to unite. For example, the data you want to use to personalize your product (Personalize, B2) might hinder the privacy-by-design guidelines you wish to follow (Preserve Data Privacy, R2). Or the special feeling someone gets from being the first to own your product (Deliver Prestige, B19) might counteract your sustainability goals (Lengthen Lifespan, B22). If you manage to unite these seemingly contradicting design strategies, you may have a winner on your hands.

○ This book can be a great source of knowledge, but it doesn't excuse you from going out into the field. Reading a slide deck about someone else's research is not enough. Any innovation process should start with developing a deep understanding of consumer needs and expectations.

○ The black pages of the book contain design principles, theoretical models developed by other innovation experts or case studies. If you want to know more, ask Google.

○ You can use design strategies to identify which design directions to explore at the start of your innovation process, as an inspirational tool in brainstorming sessions, or to find opportunities for strengthening your products' core positioning.

○ Design strategies in this book are crosslinked to each other. For example, Increase Efficiency (B10), Facilitate Sharing (B21), Lengthen Lifespan (B22), and Reduce Footprint (B23) can all improve a product's sustainability.

Download your Design Strategies Workshop Toolkit at
www.designthingsthatmakesense.com

A TYPOLOGY OF NEEDS FOR HUMAN-CENTERED DESIGN

> **Human needs specify innate psychological nutriments that are essential for ongoing psychological growth, integrity, and wellbeing[9]."**
>
> Deci and Ryan

Psychology and behavioral studies commonly create typologies to describe underlying dimensions or characteristics of peoples' behavior or needs. These typologies can in turn help us to make sense of otherwise puzzling behavior.

Desmet and Fokkinga developed a needs typology specifically for user-centered design practice and research, focused on user experience and wellbeing[6]. They identified 13 fundamental needs, carefully selected from six existing typologies, each illustrated by four sub-needs. The purpose of these sub-needs is to offer a more in-depth illustration of the fundamental needs; they are not exhaustive, nor do they apply to everyone. Sub-needs can take shape through goals and desires that are specific to particular individuals and/or situations.

The typology of needs for human-centered design is a helpful design research and practice tool. Visit the website from the Delft Institute of Positive Design for more information on designing for positive user experiences and to download a booklet on the typology of 13 fundamental psychological needs: https://diopd.org/thirteen-fundamental-psychological-needs/

Autonomy:
Being the cause of your actions and feeling that you can do things your own way, rather than feeling as though external conditions and other people determine your actions.

- Freedom of decision
- Individuality
- Creative expression
- Self-reliance

Beauty:
Feeling that the world is a place of elegance, coherence and harmony, rather than feeling that the world is disharmonious, unappealing or ugly.

- Unity and order
- Elegance and finesse
- Artistic experiences
- Natural beauty

Comfort:
Having an easy, simple, relaxing life, rather than experiencing strain, difficulty or overstimulation.

- Peace of mind
- Convenience
- Simplicity
- Overview and structure

Community:
Being accepted by a social group or entity that is important to you, rather than feeling you do not belong anywhere and have no social structure to rely on.

- Social harmony
- Affiliation and group identity
- Rooting (tradition, culture)
- Conformity (fitting in)

Competence:
Having control over your environment and being able to exercise your skills to master challenges, rather than feeling that you are incompetent or ineffective.

- Knowledge and understanding
- Challenge
- Environmental control
- Skill progression

Fitness:
Having and using a body that is strong, healthy, and full of energy, rather than having a body that feels ill, weak, or listless.

- Nourishment
- Health
- Energy and strength
- Hygiene

Impact:
Seeing that your actions or ideas have an impact on the world and contribute to something, rather than seeing that you have no influence and do not contribute to anything.

- Influence
- Contribution
- To build something
- Legacy

Morality:
Feeling that the world is a moral place and being able to act in line with your personal values, rather than feeling that the world is immoral and your actions conflict with your values.

- Have guiding principles
- Acting virtuously
- A just society
- Fulfilling duties

Purpose:
Having a clear sense of what makes your life meaningful and valuable, instead of lacking direction, significance or meaning in your life.

- Life goals and direction
- Meaningful activity
- Personal growth
- Spirituality

Recognition:
Getting appreciation for what you do and respect for who you are, instead of being disrespected, underappreciated or ignored.

- Appreciation
- Respect
- Status and prestige
- Popularity

Relatedness:
Having warm, mutual, trusting relationships with people who you care about, rather than feeling isolated or unable to make personal connections.

- Love and intimacy
- Camaraderie
- To nurture and care
- Emotional support

Security:
Feeling that your conditions and environment keeps you safe from harm and threats, rather than feeling that the world is dangerous, risky or full of uncertainty.

- Physical safety
- Financial security
- Social stability
- Conservation

Stimulation:
Being mentally and physically stimulated by novel, varied, and relevant impulses and stimuli, rather than feeling bored, indifferent or apathetic.

- Novelty
- Variation
- Play
- Bodily pleasure

STRENGTHEN

BENEFITS

24 Design Strategies to
STRENGTHEN BENEFITS

When assessing if a product makes sense to them, consumers first and foremost look for benefits that meet their needs and expectations. It is your job as an innovator to design the right benefits and make them strong enough.

Product benefits can create value for people personally by enhancing their physical and mental well-being, knowledge, skills, or social status. They can create value on a user-experience level by making things easy to use, delivering better results, and delivering pleasure, convenience, or peace of mind. They can also create value on a social or environmental level by, for instance, contributing to an inclusive society or a healthier planet.

As shown by the case studies throughout this book, most successful products rely on two or three design strategies, while other design strategies play a supporting role. This creates clarity for consumers; combining too many strategies will muddle your product's positioning and confuse consumers. In short, choose wisely and keep it simple.

Some design strategies are naturally complementary and can be easily combined to support your product's overall positioning. For example, Make it Simple (B3) and Make it Hassle-Free (B5) fit quite well together. Others, like Deliver Prestige (B19) and Lengthen Lifespan (B22), may be more challenging to combine. If you are the first in the market to unite seemingly contradictory design strategies, you could strike gold.

The design strategies to strengthen benefits can help you meet consumers' (latent) needs and outperform their value expectations. They will act as a source of inspiration throughout your innovation process.

> When consumers assess if a product makes sense to them, they first and foremost look at its benefits

B1 CUSTOMIZE

Customization allows people to modify products, services, or user interfaces to their liking. Not only does customization allow people to get what they want, it also delivers a sense of control over their product. For physical products, customization can mean configuring made-to-order products or enhancing comfort and usability by enabling in-use changes, like programming drivers' profiles in a car. For digital products, it evolves around tailoring content and interfaces, like increasing the font size in your news app.

While we often use the terms customization and personalization interchangeably, they are two distinct ideas. Both aim to create tailored products and experiences, but the ways they achieve these aims are different. Customization is a conscious action, initiated by the user. Personalization is initiated by the company, and can even go unnoticed by the user, as is often the case with AI-based personalization. For more on personalization, see Personalize (B2).

Customize to Improve the User Experience

A great way to improve the user experience for physical products is to allow people to configure their user profile. For example, when you approach your Tesla, the car recognizes your smartphone and activates your profile, complete with personal seat settings, steering wheel and mirror positions, acceleration and steering styles,

climate control and seat heating, regenerative breaking and creep, and various autopilot settings.

Fully digital products like software, websites, and apps allow you to offer endless customization possibilities at minimal costs. But just because you can, doesn't mean you should; too many options can be overwhelming and create needless complexity. "Progressive disclosure" is a popular technique in UX design to guide users through the customization process. You show the most useful customization options first, and other options in later screens. You allow people to exit the customization process at any point and continue later if they want. Popular customization features include choosing which information is shown on the home screen, turning notifications on and off, and setting an interface design. The Nest Learning Thermostat allows people to customize the screen to light up as they walk in the room and display what they want: the temperature, weather, or time. You can even choose a digital or analog clock face.

Customize to Make It Unique

Customizing products can have a positive effect on the emotional attachment people form with products and can increase brand loyalty. The time they invest in customizing the product can also lead to increased value perception. As too many options can be overwhelming, many brands offer "popular configurations" as an alternative starting point to the process, instead of customizing from scratch. Trek's Project One bikes are fully customizable. You begin by picking one of many bike families, then choose colors and design schemes, and pick your parts individually or choose a preconfigured combo. You can even put text on the frame.

To enhance the shopping experience for customized products and help consumers assess their creations, online shops are now implementing augmented reality tools, allowing you to view your product "in real life."

Customize for Physical or Mental Comfort

3D printing and robotics enables the affordable production of products made for a person's body. Using their professional scanners in retail stores, the footwear company Aetrex measures the shape, dimensions and pressures of your feet, allowing them to 3D print tailor-made insoles. Startup Wiivv does something similar, using just your smartphone's camera and an app. They use your images to produce a three-dimensional model of your feet and deliver tailor-made insoles or sandals to your doorstep.

An often-overlooked form of customization is allowing users to tailor a product's settings to accommodate for mental comfort or prevent stress. Examples are selectively muting incoming messages and setting the autopilot cruise distance between your car and the car in front of you to a distance that feels safe to you.

DOS & DON'TS

○ Nudge people to customize their products. Customization enhances the user experience, but many people are not aware of the options.

○ For physical products, keep costs down by finding the right balance between product adaptability and component standardization.

○ Don't offer too many customization options; you will scare people off. Research your users' interests and needs to identify the customization options they value the most.

B2 PERSONALIZE

Personalization entails the creation of products and customer journeys tailored for better, more individual customer experiences. Companies that recognize people by name and recommend products based on their past behavior are far more likely to retain customers. Products that adapt to their users tend to have higher customer satisfaction.

Personalization is initiated by the company behind the product. Information about designing tailored products customized by the customer can be found in design strategy Customize (B1). The following are different types of personalization you can apply in your design:

Personalize Recommendations

Netflix's recommendation engine generates personalized suggestions intended to help you bypass your genre bias. They identify similar characters or storylines, find titles involving actors and directors you like, and analyze what people with a similar watch history enjoy. These tools allow Netflix to recommend titles you wouldn't have considered yourself. One in eight Marvel Television viewers was new to comic book-based content, one in five Stranger Things fans experienced horror for the first time in Upside Down. One in seven people was new to science fiction before exploring the dark side of technology in Black Mirror. More than 80% of all shows on Netflix are discovered through recommendations[10].

Netflix creates personalized homepages for each family member, offering movies, shows, and documentaries specifically tailored to that person's interests. They use various data sources to create this homepage: what you viewed in the past, search history, genre, time, date, and which device you're on. If you like a certain actor, Netflix will choose a thumbnail that highlights that actor.

Personalize Search Results

While search results may seem general and impersonal, this could not be further from the truth. In curating your search results, Google takes many factors into account, such as search history and location. If you search for steakhouses, Google will only display steakhouses near to you. Furthermore, Google analyzes your search history clues as to which steakhouse you may prefer. If you've viewed a certain steakhouse's website or left a positive review on another, Google will give their results higher priority. What you end up getting is a curated, highly personal list of search results.

Personalize Content

During a conference in New York, Tony Jebara, head of machine learning at Netflix, explained how the platform shows their audience personalized thumbnails based on their inferred interests. As he explains about the show "Stranger Things": "Perhaps we realize you're into teenage or younger shows, so it's great for us to show you this image of two teenagers as the entry point into this show if you know nothing about it. Or if you like to watch scary horror movies, maybe we should show you the image of this slightly creepy-looking bleeding nose scene and that way intrigue you to think, oh, maybe there's something there for me as well[11]."

Netflix artwork

○ A simple way to start personalizing is to segment people into groups with similar characteristics and behavior. Later on, you can move to a more individual approach.

○ To make recommendations more trustworthy, it helps to explain why you make the recommendations. E.g., "Because you watched Black Mirror."

○ Be fully transparent with what data you are storing and what you're using it for.

○ Don't be pushy; go easy on alerts and messages.

B3 MAKE IT SIMPLE

As the world around us becomes increasingly complex, people crave simplicity more and more. This is true in every aspect of our lives, from household tasks to work routines, and entertainment to healthcare. Simplicity seems easy, yet it's likely the most difficult design strategy of all. The following are six ways to make things simpler:

Less Friction

Most customer journeys are too long and create too many points of friction. Removing or automating steps helps to produce simpler, more enjoyable customer journeys and better customer experiences. Take, for example, contactless car keys; proximity to your vehicle is all you need to unlock it. Lifesum is a digital self-care app that helps you reach your health and weight goals through better eating. Every aspect of the app was designed with simplicity in mind. For example, keeping track of calorie consumption can be done by scanning barcodes on food packages or taking a picture of your plate. Lifesum recognizes what's on your plate; all you have to do is submit how much of it you're eating.

Less Thinking

Most people appreciate it when products are simple to configure and use. For example, the Nest smart thermostat brought simplicity to climate control by removing all the buttons from

their interface and replacing them with a single dial that can be turned to adjust the temperature. Nest records temperature adjustments and programs itself based on your lifestyle, even automatically lowering temperatures when no one is home to save energy.

Less Clutter

An outstanding user experience depends on an excellent user interface. Unfortunately, many engineers, developers, and even designers place too much value upon their own opinions when designing. As they are highly knowledgeable about the interfaces they create, they often want to see more information than the average user. This leads to visual clutter and often makes the product overcomplicated for everyday users. Luckily, there are many ways to mitigate unnecessary complexity: offer people a choice in user profiles, unlock features and information as people get more experienced in using the product, or allow people to customize their interface.

More Integration

Integrating your product with the other products that people already use can help to maintain simplicity. Besides simplifying the customer journey, Lifesum also integrates with exercise apps that people are already using. They draw on the data from these apps to generate personalized lifestyle and fitness recommendations. By doing this, Lifesum can offer recommendations without complicating its own app.

More Focus

Products run the risk of becoming a multi-headed beast. They go in so many directions or implement so many features that it becomes difficult for people to understand what the product is for. While designing, keep in mind the 80/20 rule: 80% of a product's usage is due to only 20% of its features. These percentages, while not fixed, offer innovators a good guideline.

Instagram started as a web app called Burbn that allowed people to check in, share their plans, and post photos. The founders stripped Burbn of all of its features except photo sharing, liking, and commenting. They added photo filters to strengthen the app's core positioning, renamed the app Instagram, and went after the mobile photo-sharing market with full force. Since then, Instagram has retained its core focus of sharing visual media and has gained a billion users.

More Logic

Humans are hardwired to look for patterns. We grow accustomed to them and expect to find them across many applications. For example, people expect to find menus at the top of a website and at the bottom of an app. To like something, people search for a thumbs up or a heart. To refresh their timeline, they expect to "pull to refresh." Many UX Design Patterns related to data entry, color coding, content hierarchy, navigation, etc., can be specific to individual operating systems. For example, iPhones and Androids each have their own UX Design Patterns. As people get used to them, these patterns function as a lock-in; when buying a new phone, people tend to stick to the operating system they are used to.

DOS & DON'TS

○ Give people a choice of how much information they want to see.

○ Stick to UX Design Patterns, as they bring logic to the people using your product. Resist the temptation to do things too differently to stand out from the crowd.

○ Don't overdo simplicity; it might backfire. If you remove too many steps in the customer journey, people might feel they lack control or think that the service isn't personalized to their needs.

The Pareto Principle: 80% of the effect comes from 20% of causes

43

KISS

Keep It Stupid Simple
or, Keep It Simple, Stupid.

KISS is a design principle made popular by the U.S. Navy in the 1960s. It originated in aerospace design but is now used by engineers, developers and designers across all sectors. It is especially popular in software development. KISS focuses on the idea that if we can't understand a product, we can't use it properly. This is as true for mobile apps as it is for electric cars.

Simplicity is harder than it sounds. This is because the people developing your products and services are knowledgeable and tech-savvy; your customers most likely are not. Meaning, what seems simple for developers can be very difficult for consumers.

Innovation teams need to go through numerous design iterations and continuously ask themselves - and others - "How can we make it even simpler?"

KISS builds on two key principles:

O   **Simplicity should be a key goal in design.**

O   **Unnecessary complexity should be avoided.**

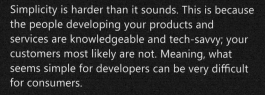

" That's been one of my mantras - focus and simplicity. Simple can be harder than complex. You have to work hard to get your thinking clean to make it simple. But it's worth it in the end because once you get there, you can move mountains."

Steve Jobs

B4 SAVE TIME

Busy lifestyles have become the new normal. People try to balance careers and active social lives, all while trying to maintain great parenting. Such hectic lifestyles drive our interest in products that promise to save time and increase productivity. To help people save time, apply one or more of the following tactics:

Do Things Faster

The premise is simple. Finishing everyday chores quicker frees up the time in our day for other things. For some of these chores, faster is already the reality. Going to the supermarket takes far more time than buying your groceries online. Nowadays, one click is all you need to add a whole shopping list to your cart. Delivery is fast; in China, supermarkets deliver your groceries within 30 minutes. Spdr also helps to speed things up. Specifically, Spdr speeds up your reading. You can use their app or their webpage to import ebooks, PDFs, and documents. Spdr then flashes that text to you one word at a time very quickly. By reading like this, you can double your reading speed.

Do Less

Outsourcing and automating tasks is one of the most valuable ways to save time and effort. Nowadays, even time-consuming tasks like preparing dinner have become as easy as making a cup of coffee. By buying pre-cut fresh meal packages at the supermarket, customers outsource meal preparation tasks to a factory. Kitchen robots—especially popular in Southern Europe—blend, mix, whip, chop, grind, and even cook entire meals in a single appliance. Moley Robotics took doing less to a whole new level by creating the world's first robotic kitchen. To design the robot, they captured the cooking techniques of Tim Anderson, the winner of BBC's 2011 MasterChef. Algorithms translated the data into elegant digital movements for the robotic arms. The robot cooks complete meals, tells you when ingredients need replacing, suggests dishes based on the items you have in stock, learns what you like, and even cleans up the cooking area afterwards.

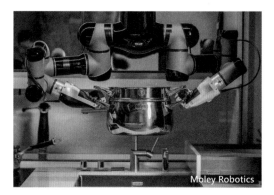

Moley Robotics

Do More Things at the Same Time

Saving time by multitasking is tricky, as research shows that multitasking can inhibit the efficiency with which individual tasks are performed. However, in some cases, it works brilliantly. For example, many people struggle to find the time to read the books they're interested in. Audiobooks enable them to cross books off of their reading list as they go about their daily activities. While audio is the new kid on the block in the publishing world, it is a rapidly growing market segment. Malcolm Gladwell's audiobook "Talking to Strangers" is outselling the print version by a factor of two[12]. The last couple of years saw more movie stars narrating novels and more VIPs reading their life stories. For example, if you have 19 free hours, you can listen to Michelle Obama reading her memoir "Becoming." Productions are becoming increasingly professional, using multiple narrators, and making use of immersive 3D audio. In the future, "authors" will exclusively write audio content as audiobooks become a category of their own.

Do Better in the Same Amount of Time

Increasing the efficient use of the time allotted to a task helps deliver better results. Grammarly is an AI-powered writing assistant that checks your writing in real time. It analyzes grammar, spelling, clarity, style, and tone. You can choose whether you want to sound neutral, confident, joyful, optimistic, friendly, urgent, analytical, or respectful. You can set your intent to inform, describe, convince, or tell a story. Grammarly uses these settings to help eliminate errors and suggest the perfect words to express yourself. It even checks for plagiarism.

DOS & DON'TS

○ The crowded market for "time saving" products and services makes it difficult to stand out. Choose a narrow target group and seek sharp consumer insights to make sure you strike the right chord.

○ Clarify how you propose to help people save time: speed things up, outsource, multitask, or improve results.

○ Be specific how much time you will help people save: number of minutes or hours, twice as fast, etc. Back your claim with data, and if possible, scientific evidence.

○ Don't design products and services that contribute to the user's stress. Your solution should offer convenience or peace of mind.

B5 MAKE IT HASSLE-FREE

Living a hassle-free life means removing irritations and inconveniences from our daily lives. The "Hassle-Free" design strategy is related to the Make It Simple (B3) and Save Time (B4) design strategies since removing steps from the customer journey and automating tasks are both effective ways to remove friction from our daily lives. Although saving time is a great side effect, the goal of "Hassle-Free" is to remove irritations and inconveniences. You can address the following five activity types to help reduce hassle in people's lives:

Things We Dislike

We postpone many household tasks just because we dislike doing them. Fortunately, we live in a time where machines can take over some of these tasks. Vacuum robots, for instance, automatically clean your floors. Litter-Robot is an automatic, self-cleaning litter box. Scooping poop is old news and a clean bed of litter now always awaits your cat. Win-win.

Things That Make Us Feel Uncomfortable

Some tasks, while not difficult or time-consuming, get put off because they make us feel uncomfortable. For example, we might avoid asking our friends for the money they owe us. Splitwise solves this. Their app makes it easy to keep track of who paid what and allows you to easily settle the expenses. They remove all awkwardness from the process.

Things That are Time-Consuming

While some things are time-consuming because they're difficult, others take time simply due to the sheer amount of work involved. Imagine, for example, trying to find a specific picture you took some time ago. This is where artificial intelligence comes to the rescue. Google Photos lets you search your pictures based on keywords like "New York City." If you've labeled people or pets, you can search for a name. Google's algorithm even detects and categorizes your pictures into people and pets, specific locations, objects, and concepts. More utilitarian searches help find screenshots, videos, collages, or movies.

Things We Need to Bring

Running from here to there, multitasking, and juggling business and social activities consume much of our mental space. Every now and then, we are bound to drop the ball and forget the things we need. Increasingly, our smartphones are helping us out. Apple Pay has replaced our wallets. Smart locks have replaced our house and car keys. Face and thumbprint recognition has made passwords a thing of the past. All we need to remember to bring is our smartphone and a charger.

Things That Must Work

We are growing increasingly accustomed to paying to use products instead of owning them. When we pay to use a product, we always expect that product to work. If it doesn't, we expect the company to immediately repair or replace it. Such practices are common in the business world but only recently became popular among consumers. With consumers now willing to pay a premium for the convenience of an always-working product, manufacturers and service providers are moving towards "Product-as-a-Service" offerings. Homie, for example, charges you for the use of household appliances like washing machines and dryers. If you choose to wash at low temperatures or run an eco-program, you pay the lowest fee, thereby stimulating sustainable behavior. Swapfiets is a Product-as-a-Service bike service: if your bike is broken, they drive by to repair it or swap it for another. For more information on Product-as-a-Service, see page 50.

Litter-Robot

PRODUCT-SERVICE SYSTEMS

As digital technologies and connected products spur innovative business models, companies no longer just sell products. Instead, they offer a combination of tangible products and intangible services: so-called Product-Service Systems (PSS).

With a PSS, the value a consumer gets is more than just that of the product they purchase. For example, the bike rental service Swapfiets adds reliability to the convenience of an electric bike. If the bike doesn't work, Swapfiets comes by to repair it on the spot or swap it for another one. Another example is Share Now. Their shared car service allows you to avoid car ownership costs by just using a car when you need one. Whim's Mobility-as-a-service offers the flexibility to travel from point A to B using different modes of transport.

PSSs offer companies several benefits. First, instead of selling a one-off product, they establish a long-term relationship with the customer. Second, they install a recurring revenue stream. Finally, they gain valuable knowledge about the customer's behavior and product usage, as well as the product's behavior during operation, both of which offer valuable innovation insights.

PSSs, especially shared services, are often attributed with positive environmental effects. As products remain owned by the company it is in their best interest to take good care of them, ensuring long lifespans. And because people share products, the total number of products decreases. Unfortunately, human behavior sometimes diminishes these positive environmental effects. Shared electric scooter services, for example, cause people to walk and cycle less, which leads to an overall negative environmental effect. Besides, people tend to treat products that aren't theirs worse than they would their own; many shared electric scooters last only months instead of years.

Right page: eight archetypical PSS business models, inspired by Tukker, 2006[13]

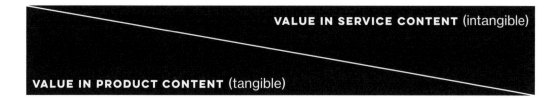

PRODUCT-ORIENTED

The business model is still mainly geared towards the sale of products, but some extra services are added.

USE-ORIENTED

The product remains under provider ownership, and is made available in a different form, sometimes shared by several users.

RESULT-ORIENTED

The consumer and company agree on a result, there is no pre-determined product involved.

Product-Related Service

Selling a product combined with a service related to that specific product. The product is owned by the customer. The customer pays a one-time fee for the product plus a recurring fee for the service. *Example: car with a maintenance contract.*

Product-Related Advice

Selling a product combined with advice on using the product in the safest, most efficient, or most effective way. The product is owned by the customer. The customer pays a one-time fee for the product plus a one-time or regular fee for the service. *Example: car with a driver course.*

Product Lease

Granting the customer exclusive use for an extended period of time while also taking care of maintenance and repair. The product is owned, maintained, and repaired by the provider. The customer pays a regular fee for a specific amount of intended product use. *Example: private-lease car.*

Product Renting or Sharing

Granting the customer exclusive use for short periods of time. There is a pool of products; customers (can) use different ones each time. The product is owned, maintained, and repaired by the provider. The customer pays for a subscription, pays per use, or a combination of the two. *Example: car sharing service.*

Product Pooling

Similar to product renting or sharing, but the product is/can be simultaneously used by multiple customers. The customer pays for a subscription, pays per use, or a combination of the two. *Example: car sharing service with integrated ride-sharing.*

Pay per Service Unit

Granting the customer exclusive or non-exclusive access to the product. The product is owned, maintained, and repaired by the provider. The customer pays for the output of the product. (pay-per-performance or pay-per-use) *Example: car with pay-per-mile.*

Outsourcing

Granting the customer exclusive or non-exclusive access to a service that makes use of a product. The product is operated by the provider. The customer pays for the service. *Example: autonomous car (taxi) service.*

Functional Result

Delivering an agreed result to the customer. The provider and/or the customer can be free to choose which product is used to deliver the result. *Example: mobility-as-a-service.*

B6 ENABLE ANYTIME, ANYWHERE

Technology has changed the way we work, learn, play, and travel in a radical way. One device is all we need to connect to anyone in the world anytime, anywhere. We now expect the same customer experience 24/7, wherever we are. The following are five ways to offer a smooth customer journey across time, place, and device:

Seamless Experience 24/7

In combination with automation and artificial intelligence, online services removed the need for a 'human in the loop'. For example, online reservation services offer a user-friendly alternative to phone reservations, give people a sense of control over the booking process, and allow people to make a booking any time. Amelia is a simple WordPress plugin that offers this functionality to any business owner, ensuring that people can book appointments and make reservations 24/7.

Seamless Experience Across Borders

In the past, local players dominated local markets. This is no longer the case due to the rise of highly scalable digital technologies. Although big tech companies have a dark side, they offer many benefits from a customer journey perspective. Now wherever they are, people enjoy the same seamless customer experience. As people know exactly what to expect, this reduces their overall stress. Until a few years ago people had no choice

but to accept being ripped off at the airport by overpaying for a taxi ride into town. Now, the Uber app can summon a taxi in 700 cities across the world, offering the same user experience and convenience everywhere.

Seamless Experience On and Offline

Online services are great as long as you have a stable internet connection. Services like Spotify or Google Maps address this problem by allowing people to download content for offline use. Just download the directions to your destination and never get lost again.

Seamless Experience Across Devices

Cloud-based services were the first to offer seamless experiences across devices. Spotify, for example, enables you to stream music in your Tesla, seamlessly switch to your smartphone as you exit your car, and switch back to your laptop when you get to the office. The desktop app even lets you control which device plays the music. Although optimized for each device, the user interfaces are very similar, adding to the feeling of a seamless experience.

Empower People to Do It Themselves

Computer vision and algorithms are the driving forces enabling everyday people to do things previously reserved for professionals. This changes the customer journey by allowing people to decide when and where they want to perform an action. The healthcare business, for example, is home to many startups focused on self-diagnosing. SkinVision is a mobile app that helps you understand your risk factors for skin cancer and keep track of your moles. Based on a photo of your mole, the app recommends if you should see a medical specialist. It offers a diagnostic tool that can be used anytime, anywhere.

Computer vision and algorithms are the driving forces enabling everyday people to do things previously reserved for professionals

DOS & DON'TS

○ Facilitate the entire customer journey, from beginning to end, anytime, anywhere, and on any device.

○ Facilitate omnichannel use as much as possible, allowing users to switch channels at any point in the customer journey. For example, the switch from a physical store to a call center agent to an online interface should allow people to continue where they left off.

○ Check local privacy rules and make sure your service complies with regulatory frameworks.

○ Don't simply copy-paste your interface to other devices. Design for optimal use on each device while maintaining your brand's core UX attributes.

B7 OFFER STRUCTURE

We all have that one extremely organized friend. Somehow they manage to have a career, maintain a social life, and look after their family, all while staying fit. The following are three ways to help people that lack this natural talent organize and structure their lives:

Present Relevant Options

Whether you're an entrepreneur or a parent working full time, maintaining a healthy lifestyle is challenging. As we become more aware of food's impact on our health and well-being, diet and meal planning apps are gaining momentum. Veganized helps you plan vegan meals and create grocery lists. Its nutrients function helps track your energy intake and provides macronutrient information for each dish. It presents you with recipes that suit you, taking your age, gender, weight, and physical activity level into account.

Provide an Overview

Many people feel overwhelmed by their busy lives. As a result, they fail to remember appointments, birthdays, and medical examinations, to name a few. Young families, in particular, struggle to plan, coordinate, and keep track of every family member's tasks and activities. Cozi helps them regain control. It is an application that helps coordinate and communicate everyone's schedules and activities. Cozi tracks grocery lists, manages to-do lists, dinner plans, and keeps the whole family on the same page.

Cozi tracks grocery lists, manages to-do lists, dinner plans, and keeps the whole family on the same page

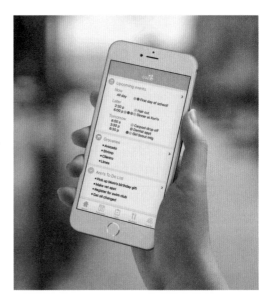

Stimulate Action

In addition to organizing your schedule and activities, mobile apps can also help you make decisions. Not only can digital calendars remind you of appointments, they can also advise you when to leave. Navigation apps like Waze help you plan better by alerting you when it's time to go, taking historical and real-time traffic data into account.

Maintain Routine

Our physical and mental health is largely dependent on a few routine behaviors. For example, we brush our teeth at least twice a day to maintain our dental hygiene. Today, technology has a growing influence on our daily routines. In 2016, Apple introduced its new Bedtime feature, which allows users to track their sleep habits and reminds them to go to bed on time. iPhone's Night Shift uses geolocation to determine when sunset is in your area. At sunset, this feature shifts the colors of your display to the warmer end of the spectrum, removing the blue light that blocks melatonin, the hormone that makes you sleepy. Combined, the Bedtime and Night Shift features prepare and remind you to maintain a healthy sleep routine.

DOS & DON'TS

○ Make information insightful and actionable.

○ People want to feel in control over their lives. Present limited options; let them decide.

○ Make your product available on different devices, including wearables.

○ Don't be prescriptive; make your product supportive of the user's life. Your product should learn from the user and adapt.

B8 GUIDE DECISION MAKING

Everyone makes thousands of small decisions every day, regardless of who they are or what they do for a living. Most are insignificant. What do you eat for breakfast? Will you have coffee, tea, or juice? Other decisions are more complex. When should you book that vacation? Should you accept that job offer? Is now the right time to move house? Fear of making the wrong decision makes us indecisive.

Technology is far better at making comparisons and analyzing huge amounts of data than humans are. The following are four ways to help people make decisions by leveraging technology:

Filter & Rank

From e-commerce platforms to search engines, many websites feature filtering and ranking tools. Although filtering and ranking generate recommendations in different ways, they usually go hand-in-hand.

Skyscanner offers a wide range of filtering and ranking options like direct flights, departure time, maximum journey duration, favorite airline, and so on. Skyscanner now also considers environmental aspects and adds the option to "only show flights with lower CO2 emissions." In case you're worried about catching a virus these days, Skyscanner can filter or rank based on a COVID-19 safety rating. This rating indicates how many measures an airline has taken to ensure passenger health safety.

Compare & Advise

The time and energy it takes to weigh options are two reasons decision making is so difficult. A clear comparison of options that highlights the recommended one can drive faster decision making and instill confidence in those decisions.

The ViaMichelin route planner displays two or three itineraries for every calculated route and allows you to easily compare travel time and costs. The "Michelin recommended" route focuses on safety, simplicity, and minimization of route errors. Customization of route recommendations is also possible. The quickest route gets you there in the least amount of time, the shortest route in the fewest kilometers. The economic route maximizes fuel efficiency and avoids toll roads, while the discovery route favors scenic drives popular for tourists.

Review & Endorse

The past decade has seen reviews become an important assessment tool. They indicate whether the product or service is a good buy and if the seller or host is trustworthy. Platforms that match sellers and buyers rely on reviews to give people the confidence to buy on their platform. Most sites allow both buyers and sellers to post reviews. Algorithms filter out any reviews that are likely to be false or automatically generated and publish the rest. Reviews range from free text format, star ratings, checkboxes, or a combination of the three. Reviewers who post often generally have a higher status, with their reviews featured more prominently. Big retailers like Amazon give detailed guidelines for writing reviews. They also allow people who are "officially associated with a product" to respond to reviews, as long as their comment complies with Amazon's guidelines.

Predict & Alert

When it comes to making purchasing decisions, we are often insecure about the right time to buy. We want to make the purchase, but we don't want to overpay.

Hopper is an airfare prediction app. Over the past 5 years, they have built an enormous database of airfare prices and pricing dynamics. By analyzing billions of prices daily, their algorithms predict how prices will change, informing users whether to book now or wait. If users decide to take Hopper's advice and wait, they can sign up for alerts that will inform them when to buy.

Structure & Guide

While the market is full of recommendation tools ready to help you make small decisions, people may be wondering how tech can help them make the big decisions. 80,000 Hours is a non-profit that offers a tool to help you decide how to best spend the 80,000 hours in your working life. The tool guides you through the decision process to find a fulfilling career. New career paths include research, government, non-profits, and more.

DOS & DON'TS

○ Be transparent about what data you use, how you use it, and ensure that your algorithms are unbiased.

○ Explain your business model and how this affects which data and options are being used as input.

○ Don't offer too many options. You want to prevent choice overload. Three is a good number.

○ Don't overwhelm users with too many filtering and ranking settings. Keep it simple and intuitive. Goal-based pre-set filter settings can be useful.

B9 SAVE MONEY

Technology helps us save money in many different ways. The Save Money design strategy focuses on minimizing costs related to purchasing decisions. Maximizing product efficiency and stimulating people to consume fewer resources will be covered in Increase Efficiency (B10).

Compare Options

Comparison websites have radically changed the way we purchase products like insurance, energy, and vacations. As digital middlemen, they help us save both time and money. However, comparison websites do have their drawbacks. Their strong focus on price fuels price wars among service providers, hotel owners, and other businesses. Additionally, these middlemen often recommend the providers that pay them the highest commission. Consumers that ignore the small print end up paying additional fees for "extras" or enter into contracts that are difficult to exit. New entrants hoping to corner the market charge a fixed fee for their services, theoretically making them more impartial. Look After My Bills uses algorithms to find you the best gas and electricity deals year-on-year. When they identify a better deal than your current one, they notify you and switch to that provider automatically. Tibber offers real-time analytics on energy usage and scans for the lowest real-time electricity prices, enabling you to buy the cheapest renewable energy at any given time. They can offer their services for a low monthly flat fee, as they also make money on selling smart home devices that can help you save even more on your energy bill.

Bundle Buying Power

Enabling people to bundle their buying power is advantageous for both the company and the customer. Customers get a better deal, and companies profit from low-cost marketing as people spread the message in their social networks. For example, organic, grass-fed meat is difficult to find and expensive. Cattle Co facilitates the creation of 'cow pools' online. People can invite others to join their cow pool by sharing the link to their personal cow pool page. Once the cow pool is fully sold, the animal is slaughtered, and pool members are invited to pick up their meat.

Automate Processes

Automating processes makes it possible to improve the customer experience while simultaneously lowering costs. The home insurance company Lemonade revolutionized the insurance business by focusing on "instant everything." They take full advantage of AI capabilities, enabling them to replace brokers and call center agents with chatbots. You can get personalized home insurance in just 90 seconds and claims are handled in seconds. Everything is app-based, eliminating the need for external paperwork. By applying technology in the right way, Lemonade keeps costs down while offering outstanding service, resulting in happy customers that save money on their insurance premium. For more information on Lemonade, see page 60.

Design for Total Cost of Ownership

Total Cost of Ownership (TCO) is the purchase price of a product plus the costs of operation (maintenance, insurance, upgrades, annual membership fees, etc.), minus the residual value (in case you sell the product before the end of its lifespan). Helping people understand your product's TCO can help them adopt a long-term view and choose the most sensible option. For example, a more expensive refrigerator might be more energy-efficient, leading to a lower total lifetime cost, even if the upfront cost is higher. Although businesses commonly think this way, individuals still tend to base their decisions on a short-term perspective. As more attention is given to environmental impact and products are offered increasingly in the form of Product-as-a-Service (see page 50), we can expect that TCO will become a more commonly used evaluation criterion among consumers.

For more information on Lemonade, see page 60.

DOS & DON'TS

O Some people link "cheaper" to "lower quality." To counter this, provide more benefits by using cost savings in combination with other design strategies.

O If you use AI to automate processes, pay close attention to Preserve Data Privacy (R2) and Offer Transparency (R3).

O TCO can scare people off as the total costs add up. Compare your solution to alternative solutions to prove that it is an economical option in the long run.

O Don't make your product too cheap; people might get suspicious. Are they getting ripped off? Is there something wrong with the product? What's the catch?

LEMONADE

Case Study

Lemonade is an app and web-based insurance company that offers policies in the US and a few European countries. Homeowner, renter, life and pet health insurance comprise their current product lineup, but it will likely expand over time. Their goal is "Instant Everything," and they use AI to achieve it. By automating processes, Lemonade's AI-driven approach lowers costs and makes the customer journey smooth, fast, and enjoyable.

Lemonade takes full advantage of AI[14] capabilities by offering people personalized insurance policies in just minutes and handling claims in just seconds. AI Maya, Lemonade's virtual assistant, collects information, provides quotes, and manages payments and billing issues. AI Jim processes claims. Simply tap the "Claim" button in the Lemonade app and tell them what happened via text chat or video message. 30% of claims are instantly approved. Lemonade predicts and catches fraud by utilizing the combined power of behavioral economics, big data, and AI. Their growing Forensic Graph Network tracks signals and analyzes relationships between things that would seem unrelated to a human. If the fraud algorithms detect a risk, the claim is passed on to a human. CX.ai, Lemonade's AI-based customer service technology, allows customers to perform actions and get answers to their questions instantly, maximizing the efficiency of their operations. And since Lemonade's customer

service team deals with fewer tickets than other insurers, they can hire the best, most empathetic agents. The result? Customers get great prices and an outstanding experience.

Another thing that sets Lemonade apart is its Giveback Policy. Lemonade pools customers together and takes a flat fee out of the pool to cover their costs. Customer claims are paid from the pool, and any remaining money is donated to a charity of that pool's choice every year. In 2020, a total of $1,128,109[15] was donated to charities.

As a B-corporation, Lemonade has been certified by the global nonprofit organization B Lab for meeting certain social sustainability, environmental performance, and accountability standards.

B3 MAKE IT SIMPLE

No paperwork; everything is app-based, from filing claims by recording in-app video messages to digital signatures.

B9 SAVE MONEY

Because everything is completely automated, costs and insurance premiums are low.

R3 OFFER TRANSPARENCY

Lemonade is transparent about how much it donates to charities every year.

Lemonade app

B1 Customize + B2 Personalize

Lemonade creates a personalized policy for you, customizable to your liking.

B6 Enable Anytime, Anywhere

No paperwork is involved. Lemonade customers can register, submit claims, upload photos, and store files using nothing more than their smartphones.

B20 Boost Social Impact

Lemonade's Giveback Policy ensures that unclaimed money is donated to the charity of your choice.

B10 INCREASE EFFICIENCY

Efficiency is doing more, with less, for longer. This applies to natural, material, informational, and energy resources. As we travel more, communicate more, and use more electronic products, our resource use increases. To counter this, we must strive to maximize product efficiency and nudge people to change their behavior.

Change the Product to Increase Efficiency

Efficiency is an important driver of innovation in almost any electronic or digital product, from cars to household appliances. For example, washing machine manufacturers are combining multiple technologies to deliver the cleanest clothes with high efficiency. Low energy and water usage are made possible by combining load-sensing technology, dirt sensors, automatic detergent dosing systems, optimized wash motions, and material innovations, to name just a few. As a result, between 1997 and 2013, the average energy consumption of the average washing machine's most efficient programs halved[16].

The Lightyear One, an electric car with solar panels integrated into the exterior, is expected to become available in 2022 and will be one of the most efficient electric cars on the market. Its five square meters of solar panels add 12 kilometers of range per hour of sunlight. The Lightyear One is about 30% more efficient than today's most efficient electric car, the Tesla Model 3[17].

Unfortunately, efficient products are usually not cheap. Educating people about the total cost of ownership can help them choose your product over cheaper, less efficient ones (see Save Money, B9).

When designing for efficiency, research the potential unintended psychological effects of your application; they can sometimes nullify the positives. Energy efficiency improvements, for example, can result in people using a product more: the 'direct rebound effect.' For example, when people upgrade from light bulbs to LED lights, they feel less guilty about leaving the lights on.

Lightyear One

Change People's Behavior to Reduce Consumption

Digital technologies are a highly scalable and cost-effective means to achieve behavioral change for the sake of resource efficiency. The following are three ways to save resources by influencing behavior:

1. Provide a Benchmark

Research shows that benchmarks can nudge people to change their behavior. The more personal a benchmark is, the more effective it will be. This is well illustrated by the reuse of towels in hotels. Towel-reuse programs that communicate with guests through neutral signs in their bathroom only have between 30% and 38% participation. Signs stating, "the majority of other guests reuse their towels" increased participation from 35% to 44%, and signs declaring that "the majority of guests in this room reuse their towels" boast a 37% to 49%[18] participation rate. Energy providers use the same principle. They use smart thermostats to benchmark your energy usage against other people with similar home and family compositions in your neighborhood.

2. Give Real-Time Feedback

Real-time feedback is a powerful behavior-changing tool; it is direct and difficult to ignore. Research shows that hotel guests who received real-time feedback on energy consumption as they showered used 11% less energy per shower than hotel guests who did not receive feedback[19]. A few gamification tactics (see page 72) could be all you need to nudge people to change their behavior.

The Toyota Prius was the first car to offer drivers real-time feedback on gasoline consumption. The dashboard showed a miles-per-gallon score, motivating drivers to beat their last "high score." This has now become a standard feature in many cars, although its effectiveness is usually diminished due to a less prominent display.

Using real-time feedback to nudge energy consumption behavior is quite common, but more can be done. While energy consumption feedback for households results in some energy savings, people still lack knowledge about the level of many appliances' energy consumption. Some startups are now addressing this challenge through "appliance fingerprinting." Every appliance has its own unique electricity usage pattern, which is like a digital fingerprint. Algorithms can detect these within an overall energy usage data stream. By connecting a single device to your smart energy meter, an app can provide you with insights into specific appliances' energy usage and send you alerts to take action. For example, if it detects that the fridge is using more electricity than usual it will send you an alert.

3. Make Predictions

For digital technologies, making predictions is the future. Predictions can significantly reduce our energy consumption. A few years from now, your electric car will function as a home battery. At the same time, your energy management system will learn from historical patterns, check your calendar, and consider weather predictions. It will then recommend when and with which energy source to charge your car. This will allow us to optimally use locally generated energy, increasing the grid's efficiency.

B11 ELEVATE PERFORMANCE

Technological performance is advancing continuously. Computers grow more powerful, ECGs more accurate, healthcare more insightful, and batteries longer lasting. As technology advances, our expectations regarding the performance of new tech products also grow. The following are six ways to improve performance:

More Speed

Just a few decades ago, people would write long reports on their typewriters. Computers have drastically quickened the writing process. Mistakes are easily fixed and can even be corrected automatically with auto-correct software. With natural language processing advancing, many people are now simply talking to their computer to "write" documents.

More Power

Some product categories like cars, power tools, household appliances, and computers place a strong focus on performance. Most product portfolios include an expensive, high-end, high-performance product to help elevate their brand's positioning. These high-performance products are usually geared for specific applications. To use computers as an example, applications include the most powerful laptop for creatives, the most powerful gaming PC, the most powerful AI server, etc.

Blendtec claims to make the most powerful blenders, and as proof, they publish the "Will it Blend" video series in which their blenders pulverize golf balls, iPhones, iPads, and the like.

More Accuracy and Precision

Sensor technology is fuelling innovation across the globe. As smart sensors grow smaller, more sensitive, and more efficient, they are being incorporated into almost everything. Wearables manufacturers are taking the lead in consumer products, allocating a large proportion of their innovation resources to improving accuracy. It is only a matter of time until smartwatches with optical heart rate monitors match chest straps' accuracy. Monitoring your heart rate 24/7 is valuable as it can help you spot stress and illness before you consciously notice it, helping you take precautionary measures in time.

More Details

This can be thought of in two ways: more breadth and more depth. More breadth, for example, can mean expanding the portfolio of measurements taken by a smartwatch. The Fitbit Versa 2 tracks not only steps and heart rate but blood oxygen saturation as well. Broadening the range of measurements recorded enables additional functionality such as activity tracking, workout intensity maps, calorie burn, stress alerts, and detailed insights into sleep stages.

More depth means increased detail within a particular element, a key innovation tactic in the audio domain. Audio has evolved from mono to stereo, to Dolby digital, to surround sound, high definition audio, and now to 3D sound. Sony launched its PULSE 3D wireless headset, fine-tuned for 3D Audio with dual noise-canceling microphones for the PS5 console, offering gamers the next generation in gaming audio.

More Duration

Batteries are a good example of innovating for improved duration. Duration, in this case, is divided into two categories. "Battery life" denotes how long you can use your device before recharging it. "Battery lifespan" denotes how long the battery itself will last before it needs replacing. Manufacturers primarily compete on battery life. With an always-on display enabled, the Fitbit Versa 2 prides itself on outcompeting the Apple Watch Series 6. Fitbit promises a battery life of up to 3 days; Apple only 18 hours. Battery lifespan is more difficult to measure, as it is affected by time, number of charge cycles, and how the battery was cared for. At some point, a battery's voltage and capacity will decrease below an acceptable threshold, a phenomenon known as battery capacity deterioration. As Apple states: "All rechargeable batteries are consumables and have a limited lifespan—eventually their capacity and performance decline so that they need to be replaced.[20]"

More Integration

More integration can lead to smaller devices and heightened functionality. Integration of components often coincides with the miniaturization of electronics, making it possible to, for example, create high-performance in-ear hearing aids that are completely invisible. Integration can also enable the creation of multifunctional devices, like hearing aids that allow users to stream music and answer calls.

DOS & DON'TS

○ Combine tactics; performance products usually excel at different types of performance.

○ Be aware that a competitive performance edge is short-lived; technology develops at lightning speed.

○ Performance products don't come cheap. Don't overdo it; even for the most affluent target groups, there is a limit to the value for money ratio.

B12 DELIGHT THE SENSES

Although humans are highly visual creatures, your design process should always take the triggering of other senses into consideration. Those senses include hearing, tasting, smelling, and feeling. One of the most effective ways to create an unforgettable customer experience is by triggering multiple senses.

Seeing

The visual aspect of a product is often our first encounter with it. It helps us recognize what the product is for, stimulates action, and evokes emotional responses. Design of the visual aspect of products can target different objectives. For example, you can design for "beauty" by applying the golden ratio, a mathematical ratio representing the most pleasing proportions a product or object can have. You can design for "today" by following color, material, and shape trends, or design for "forever" by adopting simple and sophisticated styles. You can design for "art" by making the product's visual quality more important than anything else, or for "affordances" by optimally communicating how the product should be used. For example, a design should clarify if a button needs to be pushed, pulled, or turned.

The aesthetic-usability effect dictates that, for digital products, the visual design quality directly affects our perception of usability. People perceive visually pleasing designs to be more intuitive than those they find to be less visually pleasing. Color,

balance, movement, patterns, textures, scale, shape, and visual weight can all be taken into account to create visually appealing designs. It's a time-consuming job, and your work will be judged lightning fast.

Research shows that people assess the visual appeal of a website within 50 milliseconds[21]

Hearing

Sound plays an important role in our interactions with products. Mobile phones and electric toothbrushes emit specific sounds when they need recharging. The "click" sound of a digital button in an app provides feedback that the button has been pressed, as does the "shutter sound" generated by your smartphone when you take a picture. Functionality aside, sounds can also add emotional or aesthetic value by emphasizing a product's quality, triggering a memory, or simply by being "beautiful."

As products get digitized, the design focus shifts from the sounds that mechanical movements make to the sounds we intentionally add to the product. For decades, sound design in cars centered around generating a "quality sound" when closing doors, "attention-drawing sounds" to accompany dashboard alerts, and the "performance sound" of the engine. For many people, the sound of the engine was a deciding factor in their purchase. This is changing due to the growing popularity of electric cars. The quietness of the electric motor, even while accelerating, adds to the experience of driving an electric car. This, however, introduces a whole new problem. Many pedestrians and cyclists can't hear electric cars approaching, putting them at risk. Many countries are now implementing new regulations, requiring electric vehicles to emit a combustion engine's sound when driving at low speeds. Sound can also bring joy to the customer experience. Just for fun, any passenger seat in your Tesla can "fart" whenever you want it to. Tesla is also launching customizable horn sounds.

Touching

The touch or tactile sense responds to anything that touches the skin. It helps us to experience an object's size, shape, texture, and temperature. It enables us to be precise with our motor skills.

In the past, designing for the touch sense focused primarily on physical qualities like texture, weight, shape, and movement, like the feel of pressing a button or opening and closing your laptop.

Recently, a new type of designing for the touch sense has been on the rise: haptic feedback design, or haptic UX. Smartwatches tap your wrist to signal incoming messages without alerting other people. Game controllers vibrate on one side to signal that your race car is veering off the road. Often, haptic feedback is combined with audio and visual elements to create a more powerful sensory experience.

Since Apple's 2015 release of its "taptic engine," a pun on "tap" and "haptic engine," haptic feedback and control has taken off in smartphones, tablets, and laptops. It provides tactile sensations through vibrations, while the "force touch" feature gives people more input control by distinguishing between taps and harder presses. Combined, these two features make it possible to mimic clicking a button on a flat surface.

> **Elon Musk** ✔ @elonmusk · Oct 6, 2019 ···
> Customized horn & movement sounds (coconuts being one, of course) coming to Teslas soon
>
> ○ 1.9K   ↻ 2.9K   ♡ 44.4K   ⬆
>
> **Elon Musk** ✔ @elonmusk · Oct 6, 2019 ···
> 💩 & 🐐 sounds too (also, of course)
>
> ○ 472   ↻ 566   ♡ 14.9K   ⬆

Tesla's CEO Elon Musk tweeted that new horn features, like goat noises and fart sounds, are in the making.

The tactile internet, also known as the internet of touch, is a quickly growing field. The touch sense becomes especially important if you're remotely operating robots that manipulate objects in the real world. When controlling a robot hand, you need to apply the right amount of force to pick up an object without breaking it. When performing a remote surgery, you want to feel the tissue you're cutting into. When placing a tattoo on someone's body, you want to feel the resistance of the skin so you can insert the ink at exactly the right depth.

For VR to take off, we need to be able to "feel" things in the virtual world. Think about high fiving a virtual colleague, feeling an object when picking it up, or experiencing how hard you should push a part into place when learning how to assemble a product. Sense Glove has developed a "wearable robot hand" that gives digital objects a tactile presence. Its use in VR training removes the need for expensive physical assets and makes digital prototyping more realistic.

Sense Glove

Tasting

It goes without saying that, today, people shouldn't lick their electronics. However, in the future, electronics will be designed for just that: licking and tasting. Electrodes can make people taste flavors and even simulate the sensation of having real food in their mouths.

The National University of Singapore is experimenting with a spoon embedded with electrodes that amplify the sour, bitter, and salty flavors of the real food eaten off it. This could facilitate the reduction of sodium intake in elderly people. As older people lose their sense of taste, they prefer stronger flavors and add too much salt to their food. By reducing the need for real salt, the spoon's electronic seasoning can help prevent health problems like high blood pressure.

Food, however, is not just about taste. It is also about texture and smell. The University of Tokyo is experimenting with electrodes placed on your face, directly on a jaw muscle used for chewing. As you chew your food, the electrodes can change how you experience the food's texture. For instance, it can make eating soft food feel like eating hard or chewy food. This can enhance the food experience for people with health issues that limit their ability to eat.

Smelling

For decades, inventors have been trying to use scent to enhance people's experiences. One such attempt was Smell-O-Vision, which released odor during the projection of the 1960 film Scent of Mystery. The artist Wolfgang Georgsdorf has been experimenting with a 'scent organ' for over 30 years, exposing his audiences to a symphony of smell.

Strong evidence shows that fragrances elicit emotion and are linked to emotional memory[22]. As such, they can induce fear and dislike but can also improve people's mood and sense of well-being. For example, orange and lavender have been shown to reduce the anxiety of patients in dental offices[23]. Similarly, citrus fragrances seem to have a positive effect on people who suffer from depression.

Fragrance technology hasn't taken off yet, but it will. As VR becomes more popular, any technology that enhances the virtual experience will flourish. Add smell to a virtual reality dinner with your friends, and the experience becomes far more immersive.

DOS & DON'TS

- When designing sound, consider the many aspects of that sensory experience; volume, beat, melody, repetition, pattern, and so on.

- If applied consistently, visual elements, sound, touch, and smell can become part of your brand's DNA.

- Technologies to enhance taste and smell experiences are still young. Consider if your users are open to these types of "experiments."

- Don't assume your idea of sensory delight is the same for everyone. Cultural differences cause people to enjoy contrasting sensory experiences.

B13 EVOKE JOY

Fun and entertainment are vital to stress relief. They stimulate creativity and nurture culture. For centuries, people have created ways to entertain themselves, from jesters to Lego sets. Just as they are changing other aspects of life, new technologies are changing the way we entertain ourselves. Fun and entertainment can be a product's core purpose or added to enhance a user's experience. While trying to pack their products full of benefits, innovators tend to overlook adding fun elements. The following tactics help to add a bit of fun to your product:

Make It a Surprise

As soon as something happens unexpectedly or in a way you didn't foresee, you experience surprise. Surprises, whether positive or negative, supercharge our emotions. Positive surprises make us feel happy or joyful, while negative surprises make us feel desperate, angry, or unhappy[24]. If done right, the addition of surprise to your customer journey can increase customer satisfaction and engagement.

Years ago, TED talks introduced their "Surprise Me" feature, claiming to "deliver serendipity on demand." Many companies offer personalized gift vouchers on your birthday or a thank you discount for keeping everything from your last online order. All these little surprises can easily be programmed into the customer journey but tend to have a commercial feel. In practice, nothing beats a random act of kindness, which is a kind of surprise that technology cannot yet cater to.

Make People Curious

"Over the last year, the tech product that has brought the most joy into my life has undoubtedly been Discover Weekly, Spotify's playlist of tracks personalized for my taste," remarks an editor of "The Verge[25]." The Discover Weekly playlist is Spotify's algorithmically personalized playlist of 30 songs brought to you every Monday, offering various artists to explore. Following its success, Spotify launched Release Radar. Every Friday, Spotify displays new releases from artists you've listened to and follow. Both playlists are hugely popular and serve to trigger listeners' curiosity twice a week.

Make It Playful

Making products more playful can increase user engagement. Simple animations can make your interface come to life in fun to explore ways. IKEA enhances your shopping experience in a playful way. Through the IKEA Place app, AR on your smartphone previews how that new couch would look in your living room in different colors and configurations. Headspace uses funny icons and lighthearted language to take the seriousness out of meditation and make it accessible to everyone. Although western societies accept and appreciate playfulness in digital interfaces, we tend to prefer a more serious hardware design. On the other hand, in Asia playful hardware is far more appreciated. Robot design makes this very apparent. Robots designed in Europe and the US are humanoids that appear to have come straight out of a science fiction movie, while robots designed in Japan or China tend to have light colors, round shapes, and friendly heads with happy expressions.

Make People Smile

A little humor can have a big effect, strengthening the bond people feel with your product. If it's been a while since you've opened Tinder, you'll receive a funny alert to persuade you to check it out.

Tesla hides 'Easter eggs' in their software updates: fun features for users to discover. Usually, they are well hidden, which adds to the fun. They're a great way to engage drivers and let the Tesla team show they enjoy having a little fun every once in a while. For example, the artist's sketch pad lets you submit your sketch to Tesla. If you tap "publish," it asks: "Are you sure you want Tesla to critique your artistic masterpiece?" You can choose from two options: "No, the world isn't ready for my art," or "Yes, I am an artist!" This kind of interaction helps to increase brand engagement.

Make It a Game

Gamification is a tactic that excels at making your product more fun. See page 72 for gamification tactics.

DOS & DON'TS

O Surprise is a double-edged sword because it intensifies emotions, both positive and negative. Make sure to test it on a large number of people before launch to make sure it has a positive effect.

O Don't overdo it; even a tiny positive surprise has a major effect, albeit temporary. A study discovered that people who found just a dime showed higher overall satisfaction with life than people who did not find a coin[26].

GAMIFICATION

Gamification applies "game mechanics" to non-game contexts. Although the term "gamification" is derived from the word "game," it is not about entertainment. Instead, gamification makes use of game design elements to increase people's motivation and engagement.

While it is people's intrinsic motivators that initially attract them to your product, extrinsic motivation keeps drawing them back. Gamification principles can help your design offer extrinsic motivation.

A universal classification of gamification elements does not exist. Although there are more, most products build upon a foundation of three game elements: points, badges, and leaderboards[27]. The gamification elements on the right page can serve as building blocks in your product design. Be selective; you don't have to include them all.

Points
Numerical indicators for progress.
Examples: scores, experience points, budget.

Badges
Visual icons that represent achievements
Examples: medals, trophies.

Leaderboards
Leaderboards show people's ranks within the community for comparison.
Examples: rankings and scoreboards.

Progression
Visual or numerical progress indicators.
Examples: milestones, streaks, status bars.

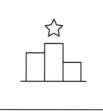

Status
Text labels or visual icons that indicate progress.
Examples: titles, ranks.

Levels
Levels indicate a hierarchy of increasingly difficult environments
Examples: challenges, stages, worlds.

Rewards
Valuable gifts and desirable items linked to achievements like earning badges or finishing levels.
Examples: incentives, prizes, gifts.

Roles
Elements of a character.
Examples: class, avatar.

B14 SHAPE MEMORIES

Technology allows us to go places and do things that are out of reach in our daily life. Smartphones, along with AR and VR, are wonderful tools that enhance experiences, refresh old memories, and create new ones.

Refresh Old Memories

Sometimes, a simple trigger is all it takes to refresh your memory. Take the "Memories" feature on your iPhone. It triggers the rediscovery of moments that are saved in your photo library. Memories are collections of pictures clustered around people, places, and events. The feature also helps to frame your memories, creating movies out of your pictures, and sharing them with family and friends.

VR is an increasingly popular tool in the fight against loneliness. Rendever offers customized reminiscence therapy tools that take elderly people with dementia on a stroll down memory lane by revisiting their childhood home, wedding location, or other significant locations from their past. Rendever's VR platform can even draw people out of expressive aphasia, as they demonstrate in an online video of Mickey[28].

Mickey's caregivers were unable to bring her out of her shell until she found VR. As soon as she found herself in a room full of virtual puppies, she began to speak and laugh, expressing tremendous joy.

Rendever VR glasses

Create New Memories

VR is an excellent memory creation tool, as it can teleport you to anywhere in the world. Visiting Paris for the first time, soaring in the air above the Sahara, or enjoying roller coasters—with VR, all of this is possible. This, too, can add some excitement to the lives of the elderly. VR GENIE is a project from Equality Lab that aims at fulfilling seniors' last wishes through immersive technology.

At the other end of the age spectrum, Google Expeditions teaches kids around the world in an awe-inspiring way. They offer over 1000 VR and 100 AR tours. Kids can virtually explore museums, swim with sharks, navigate outer space, and much more without ever leaving the classroom. Using AR, Google Expeditions bring abstract concepts to life.

You can see and walk around 3D objects as if they were physically there and choose from numerous 360° scenes.

Casa Batlló, a house designed by Antoni Gaudí, offers visitors an enhanced multimedia tour. Visitors are given a smartphone-like device with AR functionality. Pointing the camera at any part of the room triggers the screen to display computer-generated graphics overlaid onto the real environment, giving an impression of how the room was originally decorated. Pointing at certain objects reveals Gaudi's source of inspiration. For example, a mushroom is projected onto the fireplace's halo to reveal Gaudi's inspiration from nature.

DOS & DON'TS

○ Expect numerous tests and iterations to get it right. It's about hitting exactly the right chord and triggering the right emotions.

○ Today's VR glasses are clunky and uncomfortable, and most people have not yet experienced immersive VR. Keep it short; many people need a break after 15-30 minutes.

○ Don't make it a gimmick. The novelty will soon wear off, leaving your product or feature unused.

B15 STIMULATE LEARNING

Many people strive to enhance their personal or professional abilities by improving their knowledge and developing skills. The arrival of online learning and mobile apps has increased our learning opportunities tremendously. Now, we can learn at our own pace, whenever we like, wherever we like. Prerecorded videos, live webinars, podcasts, peer-to-peer platforms, chatbots, and VR experiences; the possibilities are endless. While online education was regarded as lower quality in the past, acknowledgment of online degrees and certificates by educational institutions and employers is growing. Technology helps us make learning faster, more effective, and more engaging. Here are some different ways to stimulate learning:

Make It a Learning Journey

Some people who would like to learn a new knowledge or skill just don't know where to start. By making learning a guided journey, you can lower the threshold for people to get started. The meditation app Headspace invites you to take three consecutive basic courses, each made up of 10 short sessions. These courses introduce you to mindful meditation and help acquaint you with their style of teaching. Although it's not compulsory to complete the basic levels before moving on to other courses, they do encourage it.

Make It Rewarding

Gamification is an excellent way to keep people engaged (see page 72). The language app Duolingo excels in applying gamification techniques with their daily goals, compliments, and awards. They make learning a new language interactive and fun, getting rid of boring vocabulary and grammar drills. Data from tens of millions of active users help them level up difficulty without overwhelming people.

❝ **We prefer to be more on the addictive side than the fast-learning side. If someone drops out, their rate of learning is zero[29].** ❞

Luis von Ahn, CEO of Duolingo

Make It Social

Peer-to-peer learning is on the rise. In a school setting, it is students teaching other students, in the workplace employees teaching other employees. Besides getting access to a community of people who can help you out, you also learn a great deal from teaching others. Brainly calls themselves the "24/7 homework helper." It's a knowledge-sharing community that gives students access to millions of previously answered homework questions and allows them to ask "experts." Students can earn points to spend asking their own questions by answering other users' questions.

Make It Personal

Everybody is unique. Our strengths, weaknesses and learning speeds all differ. While human teachers tend to pick up on this intuitively, AI is the digital world's equivalent. Educational chatbots are on the rise, especially in language learning apps. But technology still needs to advance further before we reach voice recognition and virtual teachers that will add "personal touches" to digital learning.

Make It Accessible

Online platforms make learning opportunities widely available and accessible to anybody. Founded by Harvard and MIT, EdX is an online learning platform that offers courses from over 160 universities. Their mission is to make high-quality education accessible for everyone, everywhere. You can take courses for free or pay a small fee for assessments and a certificate.

For those who find university-level courses too in-depth, Udemy might be an alternative. Their courses are created by "normal people." As a result, their marketplace offers something for everyone.

Make It an Experience

As immersive experiences help us understand and remember, AR and VR will change the way we learn. Currently, numerous startups are entering the field of AR/VR learning. Still, Google Expeditions is lightyears ahead with their vast number of AR/VR tours for kids. If you want to teach kids about astronomy, nothing beats a virtual trip to outer space. Besides enabling exploration of the real world in a virtual way, e.g., visiting the Eiffel Tower, VR and AR can bring abstract concepts like the inner workings of a volcano or the human body to life.

Make It Hands-On

Learning-by-doing and active learning are increasingly popular methods of actively involving the learner in the learning process. Google Expeditions Tour Creator enables students to create their own VR tours using images from Street View. By creating their own tours, students learn much more about a location than just following ready-made tours.

Senstroke united the digital and physical worlds by creating sensors to attach to your drumsticks and your feet, allowing you to learn to play drums when and wherever you want. Their technology reproduces the drumsticks' impact for a realistic feel. You can play, record and progress at your own speed thanks to the learning mode that's built into the application.

B16 PROVIDE INSIGHT

Gaining insight into your behavior, performance, health, and environmental conditions is the first step towards becoming a "better you." Benjamin Franklin, one of the Founding Fathers of the United States, was a pioneer in what today we call the "quantified self movement." Franklin embarked on a "bold and arduous project of arriving at moral perfection," as he wrote in his autobiography[30], tracking 13 life virtues. By actively trying to improve one specific virtue every week, and using pen and paper to track his progress, he was about 250 years ahead of his time. Today, we use wearables and other data sources to track our activity as a means to gauge our physical and mental states. This helps us to understand, for example, why we are overweight, why we feel sluggish, and what affects our mood. We gain self-knowledge through self-tracking. In the past, we asked our doctors. Today, we can ask our data. The following are four ways to help people gain insight:

Insight Through a Metric

If you succeed in making it incredibly simple for people to gain insights through data, you'll create fans. An increasingly popular way to do this is by creating a unique metric: a single number representing people's overall performance. Weight Watchers provides a prime example: they take nutritional data like the number of calories and the amount of protein, sugar, and saturated fat and translate this varied information into a single number called the SmartPoints value. People joining the program get a specific amount of Daily SmartPoints based on their age, height, weight, and sex to ensure that they reach their weight-loss goal. They also get extra weekly SmartPoints when they really need them, like on their night out with friends.

Insight Through (Real-Time) Measurements and Alerts

Technology allows us to measure and track our stress levels, heartbeat, blood pressure, and many more things, and alert us when something needs our attention. An Apple Watch checks for unusually high or low heart rates and gives an alert if these occur when you appear to have been inactive for more than 10 minutes. Alerts can also be triggered upon detection of irregular heart rhythms, which can prompt the app to recommend that you consult a medical specialist. All this on-going data is constantly logged in the Health app to be viewed at any time.

Insight Through Data Visualization

People are visual creatures. We process images much faster than text, and images can therefore help us understand data more clearly. As we collect more and more data about ourselves, data visualization becomes increasingly important for people to make sense of it. Some smart tech products take data visualization far beyond graphs. The Naked Labs Body Scanner, for example, is a scale combined with a smart mirror that uses infrared light to capture a 3D model of your body, which is then rendered on the Naked app. Not only does it help you analyze historical data (regarding weight, fat percentage, lean mass, fat mass, and more) through detailed charts and graphs, but you can literally watch your body change. Side-by-side comparisons of your 3D body model allow you to see progress in a whole new way.

Insight Through Comparison

Seeing your data is one thing; understanding what it means is another. One way to help people understand their data is by comparing it to people similar to them. Using a Fitbit device with heart rate tracking, you can track the sleep stages you cycle through at night: from light sleep to deep sleep, back to light sleep, and then into REM sleep. Then the cycle repeats, assuming you sleep well. The app shows you how your sleep stages from the previous night compare to the averages of others who are of the same sex and within the same age range. You can also compare your data from last night to your own 30-day average.

DOS & DON'TS

○ Remain transparent about the data you collect and what you use it for.

○ Provide insights, but recognize that this alone is not enough; combine this design strategy with other design strategies like Fuel Motivation (B17) or Increase Efficiency (B10).

○ Give the user control over alerts and notifications (the ability to turn them on or off or adjust thresholds, for instance).

○ Don't try to do everything. Start with a single, clear focus, like helping people sleep better or reducing stress levels.

Seeing your data
is one thing;
understanding what it
means is another

B17 FUEL MOTIVATION

"I don't have time for that now." "I'll do it tomorrow." These phrases are all too familiar from our day-to-day lives. We often disappoint ourselves by planning to do something, only to lack the motivation to make it happen. Such roadblocks must be considered in the design process. Designing with motivational mechanisms in mind can help people overcome this mental barrier, change their existing habits, and achieve new goals. The following are four helpful motivation tactics:

Make It Competitive

Almost nothing drives motivation like competition. Whether you compare results with strangers or are actively competing with your peers, the desire to come out on top is a fierce motivator. This is why Apple Watch, Fitbit, and many other wearable devices push users to invite friends and family to challenges. Below are just a few of Fitbit's challenges:

Daily Showdown: Who can get the most steps today?

Weekend Warrior: Who can get the most steps over the weekend?

Workweek Hustle: Who can get the most steps Monday through Friday?

Goal Day: How many participants can reach their daily step goal?

Family Faceoff: Which member of your Fitbit family account can get the most steps Monday through Friday?

Adventures: Choose between non-competitive solo journeys or challenge friends to the finish line across real life locations.

Make It a Goal

One effective way to kickstart behavior change is by setting goals that are ambitious but still doable. The satisfaction you feel after achieving a goal motivates you to continue working toward the next one. Getting in shape, learning a new skill, and even personal growth begin with that first goal you set. A goal tracking app like Coach. me helps you do this and supports you along the way. It records when your activities contribute to your goal by aligning with the habits you hope to build. To deliver the "motivational pressure" you need to continue, the app provides daily reminders, community support, and advice from real coaches.

Make It Rewarding

One of the main factors motivating people to continue pursuing their goals is noticeable progress. A continued sense of achievement along the way helps make the end goal seem more attainable. For example, while losing fifty pounds may seem like an impossible task, that one-pound difference on the scale every week gives people the confidence that they can attain their goal weight if they continue. Earning points and badges while pursuing the goal is a strategy proven to deliver people the motivation they need to keep raising their performance to the next level.

These days, badges, achievements, and trophies are baked into our daily routines. They encourage productivity, motivate workouts, and incentivize mindfulness. Headspace is a popular meditation app that gives positive reinforcement in the form of meditation milestones, badges, celebratory banners, and publicly shareable stats. Gamification techniques like these help motivate users to continue their daily meditation activities.

Make It Fun

Many people struggle to translate their good intentions into action, even if physical exercise is not involved. Meditating for just a few minutes a day may sound easy, but most people tend to put it off when the time comes. Headspace found a way to nudge users in a fun, light-hearted way. They motivate users with happy suggestions, cheerful visuals, and a bit of humor.

❝ While health can be serious business, we feel it doesn't have to be. We believe you're more likely to reach your goals if you're encouraged to have fun, smile, and feel empowered along the way[31]. ❞

Fitbit

DOS & DON'TS

○ Use gamification tactics to engage and motivate people. See page 72 for an overview of gamification tactics.

○ Goals are motivating if they are both ambitious and doable. Encourage people to keep going if they regularly meet their goals; suggest setting more achievable goals if they don't.

○ Developing new habits is difficult enough in itself, so make sure that your product is simple and easy to use. An intuitive user interface design is key; some humor might help.

○ Don't overdo it; nudges and notifications can easily be overbearing. The goal is to motivate, not to annoy.

FITBIT

Fitbit is the remarkable story of two founders who made a fortune pioneering wearable fitness trackers with no prior electronic manufacturing experience.

In 2007, Fitbit founders Eric Friedman and James Park realized that sensors and wireless technology had advanced to a point where they could revolutionize fitness and health. Their first product, now called "Fitbit Classic," launched in 2009. It could be clipped on to your clothing and required a particular wireless base station and special software to upload data to Fitbit's online portal. After a few years, they developed the first Fitbit that could directly sync with a smartphone. Fitbit was the unrivaled king of fitness trackers until 2015, when Apple launched the first Apple Watch. It took Fitbit years to respond with their own smartwatch. Although their smartwatches match Apple in functionality and undercut them in price, Fitbit never managed to overtake Apple in this segment of the market.

Fitbit's success story wasn't a smooth ride. Products were recalled because they caused allergic skin reactions. Accounts were hacked, and privacy scandals erupted when users found they had shared their activity data within the community without knowing it. Fitbit data was used as evidence in court cases, and they are currently being sued by a competitor. As one of their founders put it, "Seven times we were close to death[32]." Nevertheless, Fitbit became a massive success by making fitness a social, gamified experience. Google's 2019 acquisition of Fitbit for $2.1 billion opened the door to future competition with Apple in the smartwatch category.

Here, we'll take a look at the Fitbit Sense, Fitbit's most innovative product. It promises to deliver "The innovative features you need for a healthier life, all on your wrist." Sense also includes features that are no longer innovative and no longer unlock new value for consumers; designers call these features "dissatisfiers." Customers don't ask for dissatisfiers but will be disappointed if your product doesn't have them. For smartwatches, these include activity tracking, measuring heart rate, water resistance, do not disturb mode, always-on display mode, call/ text/ app notifications, receiving calls, and a user-friendly smartphone app. Over time, the features mentioned on the right page will also move to the "dissatisfier category" as new, more desirable features emerge.

B16 PROVIDE INSIGHT

Insight into everything you expect a smartwatch to track, including sleep stages, sleep score, blood oxygen levels, nighttime skin temperature and breathing rate, and electrodermal activity to indicate stress.

B11 ELEVATE PERFORMANCE

Up to 6+days of battery life, or up to 12 hours with GPS activated. Realistically speaking, the battery life is up to 3 days, which is still far longer than the Apple Watch 6 (up to 18 hours). 12 minutes is all it takes for a full charge with fast charging.

R6 ENSURE COMPATIBILITY

Works with Android phones, iPhones, Alexa, and Google Assistant.

Fitbit Sense

B24 Unleash New Value

Set your Fitbit alarm to wake you with a quiet vibration during a lighter sleep stage to help you feel more refreshed.

B3 Make it Simple

Everything can be found in the Fitbit app (Apple Watch requires using both the Watch app and the Health app). Voice control adds simplicity.

B17 Fuel Motivation

Fitbit's multitude of social challenges and powerful gamification tactics boost motivation, and their messages nudge behavior.

B18 DRIVE SOCIAL INTERACTION

Social interactions are exchanges between two or more individuals, and they're a crucial part of how society operates. How and what people exchange, the interpretation of what others mean, and how they act and react within the exchange, are all elements of a social interaction. Social interactions can be accidental (not planned and probably not repeated), repeated (not planned but occurring from time to time), regular (not planned yet very common), or regulated (planned and regulated by laws and legislation).

The following are the five most common forms of social interaction your product might facilitate:

Exchange

Social exchange theory explains social interaction in the context of an exchange where people try to maximize benefits and minimize costs. If the balance is off, the relationship will, at some point, come to an end. This balance, however, is an individual assessment. Your friend might be a bit cheap, but since she's always there for you when you need her, you may not mind paying for more than a fair share of the drinks. Someone else might judge her as a freeloader and think you would be better off ending the friendship. The underlying concept of exchange is reciprocity: if you do something for someone, that person owes you something in return.

Social networks have redefined the ways in which—and with whom—we interact. In social networks there is little one-to-one reciprocity (direct reciprocity); they rely on reciprocity within communities (indirect reciprocity). Thumbs up, applause and comments have become a way to demonstrate and receive appreciation from your social "friends." Kudos brings this phenomenon to the workplace with its employee recognition, feedback, and organizational communication platform. Kudos helps team leaders to recognize and reward employees, and employees to appreciate, recognize, and congratulate each other. Points and rewards can be added to strengthen the program.

Competition

Competition occurs when two or more people pursue a mutual goal that can't be shared. People compete for power, jobs, fame, status, money, luxury goods, and other scarce things.

Crowdsourcing platforms like DesignCrowd use competition to facilitate matching supply and demand. Anyone can create a competition to design a book cover, logo, app, website, or magazine. You upload a brief, define a prize, and wait for designers from all over the world to respond. Once you choose the winner, they get paid, and you get the files.

Conflict

Conflict is a clash between opposing forces, possibly involving violence. Conflicts can be about resources, power, or opposing ideas, beliefs, interests, and principles. Conflict is related to—and can result from—competition. Whereas competition is primarily about two people fighting for the same goal, conflict is strongly focused on defeating the opponent.

Algorithms are being developed that can detect a fight between lovers minutes before it actually happens. By tapping into physiological, linguistic, and acoustic data from wearables and smartphones, one learns to recognize patterns and detect an upcoming fight. A suggestion to take a walk might prevent it from happening, or bring awareness that allows things to unfold in a less confrontational way.

Accommodation

Accommodation is a form of social interaction in which people with competing or conflicting interests adjust their relationship to reach a balance. In other words, accommodation is a resolution of conflicts. Parties involved might reach a compromise by both giving-and-taking a bit, or they might ask an independent third party to mediate an agreement.

Algorithms for mediation, arbitrage, and litigation are immature but are developing at lightning speed. In China's internet courts, millions of legal cases regarding internet trade issues, copyright cases, and disputes over online product sales are handled by non-human judges powered by artificial intelligence. Citizens use video messaging to communicate with these virtual judges and receive court decisions via text messages or popular messaging services like WeChat. Officials say that human judges observe the process and

can intervene. Although it is unclear to what extent humans are still involved, what is clear is that these systems ease humans' workload and improve the speed and effectiveness of the legal process.

Cooperation

Cooperation occurs when two or more people work or act together. It is a crucial building block of society: without cooperation, we would only be a collection of individuals. For cooperation to flourish, there needs to be an overlap of goals, interests, and/or desires. Cooperation is more likely to happen if people know each other.

Tools like Slack, Workplace from Facebook, and MS Teams facilitate collaboration between remote team members. They offer everything distributed teams need, from communication tools to file sharing to planning.

B19 DELIVER PRESTIGE

Humans have always had methods of establishing and communicating social status. As technology has changed, so have these methods. Therefore, it should come as no surprise that tech products are now used as a means to express who we are or display who we want to be.

Status is a relative concept; the things that define it can differ per social group. Typically, social status is linked to items that are in some way exclusive or scarce. Many social groups have concluded that owning the latest smartphone is a status symbol, though this is not the case for all. For instance, using the same phone for as long as possible adds to your status within environmentally conscious groups, whereas owning a retro phone adds value as a lifestyle statement within other groups. The following are ways to design tech products that contribute to people's social status:

Exclusive to Circumstance

This type of exclusivity is circumstantial. It could depend on where you live, who you buy from, or which memberships you have. Amazon, for example, makes specific products available only to Amazon Prime members. People who are not a member of Amazon Prime cannot see the 'Add to Basket' button on the Prime-exclusive product's detail page. Amazon also offers exclusive movies and series, making a membership the only way to access some of its most popular shows.

Exclusive in Time

Some people just like to be first. They feel special when they get something before all their peers. Amazon First Reads offers customers early access to upcoming ebooks from Amazon Publishing. Spotify made their free accounts invite-only when launching in the US, allowing users to join only through an invitation from a friend or from Spotify. This strategy allowed Spotify to manage high levels of consumer demand and guarantee the quality of service. It was also a smart marketing strategy: let users do the marketing for you and offer those who can't get free access the option to sign up for a premium paid account at any time.

Exclusive to the Ones Who Can Afford It

People typically purchase luxury goods for emotional reasons. They hope to achieve a feeling of accomplishment, gain acceptance from others, or raise their self-esteem. When the original iPhone was released in 2007, its high price tag made it an immediate status symbol. At that time, $599 for a phone seemed outrageous. Nowadays, the top-of-the-line iPhone costs $1,600, and Samsung's Galaxy Fold has reached the $2,000 mark.

Scarce After Launch

Due to production limitations, innovative electronic products are often scarce in the first months after launch. Such scarcity can make products even more desirable. When Apple first released the iPhone, hundreds of people spent days camping outside of Apple stores across the US in an attempt to get their hands on one. Whether intentional or not, Apple managed to turn this into a cultural phenomenon, and now every subsequent iPhone release has been marked by Apple fans sitting exhausted on their lawn chairs outside Apple stores days before the release. When the iPhone X was released for preorder online, it sold out within minutes. That left millions of unlucky customers with a choice: wait four-to-five weeks for their iPhone to be delivered or wait in line at least a day in hopes of buying one of the scarce handsets available in stores.

Scarce in Number

Limited editions have long been successful in fashion, home accessories, and car businesses. Increasingly, they are being applied to consumer electronics. Sony has excelled at using the limited edition tactic with their PlayStation consoles. These limited edition consoles fall into three categories: special game editions like Spiderman or Kingdom Hearts, celebrating special moments like PlayStation's 20th anniversary or 500 million PlayStation consoles sold, or luxury design editions like consoles with a golden finish or a steel black case.

DOS & DON'TS

O Evaluate your strategy from a moral standpoint. Many consumers who buy luxury goods can't really afford them. Indulging in retail therapy can have negative long-term effects on their lives.

O Try to build status on more than novelty alone, as novelty quickly wears off. Other forms of status can create emotional attachments to products, resulting in prolonged product lifetimes.

O Don't stimulate overconsumption. It might be good for business if consumers discard products before the end of life, but it damages the environment.

Some
people just
like to be first

B20 BOOST SOCIAL IMPACT

Social impact is about the bigger picture: how can your product contribute to a better world? In the past, designing for social impact was something done mainly by non-profits. These days, a growing number of startups and commercial organizations are actively pursuing a positive social impact. For some, it is a core purpose, and for others, a positive side effect. The following are five ways to boost social impact:

Design for Equity and Equality

While both equity and equality aim to give everyone access to the same opportunities, they differ in how they achieve this. Equity is recognizing that people have unequal starting positions and correcting that imbalance. Equality is treating everyone exactly the same. Predictive Hire uses AI to remove unconscious bias from the hiring process's initial stages. Their chatbot-enabled blind interviewer solutions give everyone a fair and equal chance at the job. At Ecole42, anyone above 18 interested in coding can apply to be educated for free as a software engineer. They don't require grades, GPA, recommendations, or financial means; if you pass the full-time 4-week coding challenge, you're in. Their peer-to-peer philosophy makes every student a teacher, further contributing to a "culture of equality."

Design for Inclusivity

Inclusive design ensures that your product can be used by as many people as possible, regardless of physical or mental abilities, religion, gender, sexual orientation, or age. Unintended, non-inclusive designs can be hurtful for entire societal groups. For example, some hand dryers only work for white people, simply because the product was not tested on people with darker skin colors. Non-inclusive designs are often the result of non-diverse innovation teams. Apple's majority male development teams were blamed for ignoring women's needs when period-tracking was not initially included in their health app.

AI deserves our special attention within design for inclusivity. As the datasets used to train algorithms are often biased, large-scale AI use can easily lead to less-inclusive societies. For example, the varied accuracy of facial recognition software for skin colors and gender can lead to systematic discrimination. Offering transparency about AI is a prerequisite for a fair and inclusive society. See page 122 for more information.

Design for Accessibility

Accessibility ensures that you accommodate the needs of specific groups of people, regardless of human ability, experience, or resources. Examples include designing a car so that disabled people can easily get in and out, removing jargon from online systems to make them easier for non-native speakers, making privacy terms easy to understand for the average consumer, and enabling the visually impaired to enlarge fonts and buttons in apps.

Natural Language Processing technology promises product interaction equally easy for children, adults, and elderly people to use, welcoming even the illiterate.

Designing for accessibility is highly relevant in developing countries. Healthy Entrepreneurs uses simple technology to make basic healthcare available to people in remote areas. They offer training to entrepreneurs and equip them with a solar-powered tablet to educate their clients, promote new products, and order new stock. While the entrepreneurs make an income, basic healthcare becomes accessible in remote areas.

Design for Data Donation

What if you would use the data you collect for good? By sharing anonymized data with research institutions or making it publicly available, you could help slow global warming, reduce inequality, or fight diseases. Apple's Research app allows people with an Apple Watch and iPhone to contribute to groundbreaking research studies. The DNA analysis company 23andMe invites its customers to "become part of something bigger." Once users agree to participate in online surveys, researchers can study topics and make new scientific discoveries by linking genetic data.

DOS & DON'TS

○ Make a social impact because you believe it is the right thing to do. Think purpose, not marketing.

○ Make sure your team is diverse; diverse teams are better at designing products with social impact.

○ Explore business models of successful social ventures. Sometimes, the combination of a limited company and a foundation makes sense (it makes you eligible for different funding types).

○ Don't focus on the financial part of the business case too much. The costs are easy to measure; social return on investment is not.

B21 FACILITATE SHARING

While shared resources are not a new phenomenon, the rise of the internet and online platforms have taken this practice to a whole new level. With the click of a button, you can now share things with people you've never met before. Sharing is quickly becoming the new owning. Although sharing resources often has a beneficial impact on the environment, it also increases demand. For example, people who do not own a car might start using one regularly. The following tactics use sharing to benefit consumers:

Barter

Bartering is a fantastic way to acquire or experience new things without spending a penny. SharedEarth connects landowners to gardeners and farmers who don't have the space to start their own home fruit and vegetable garden. In exchange for free access to land, gardeners share the products they grow with the landowner.

Bartering doesn't have to be one-on-one; it works between communities as well. For example, CouchSurfing serves a global community of 14 million people in over 200,000 cities. The use of their site is entirely free, and hosts are forbidden to charge travelers. They encourage hosts to share their lives and worlds with guests, making travel a truly social experience. CouchSurfing operates on the principle of community reciprocity: you surf someone's couch, and in return, you let someone else surf yours. This works well if the services exchanged are interchangeable, and

those involved form a strong community. When it comes to goods, which often significantly differ in value, an extra mechanism must be put in place: points or money. For example, the Listia platform lets people earn credits by giving away things they no longer want and then using these credits to acquire "new things" in online auctions. Such credit systems support community bonding and keep bargain hunters out. However, to attract more users, most platforms, like Listia, eventually make it possible to buy and sell credits for money. By doing so, they turn into a platform for buying and selling items.

Borrow and Lend

The last decade saw the rise of platforms built to facilitate borrowing and lending within communities, like Peerby and Fat Llama. These platforms soon realized that they couldn't grow beyond altruistic consumers without the option for a paid service. They now offer people a choice between renting their stuff out for a fee or lending it to someone for free. Borrowing and lending are also happening on platforms built for other purposes, like Nextdoor's neighborhood platform and Facebook's social media platform.

Rent (Out)

The use of a product in exchange for money can be described by two models: peer-to-peer and operator-driven. The peer-to-peer model offers a marketplace that facilitates transactions between individuals. One such marketplace is Snappcar, whose mission is to reduce the number of cars on the road. They enable car owners to easily and safely rent out their vehicles to other people and even facilitate insurance. For those people who want assurance that a car is available near their home, Snappcar teamed up with leasing companies to offer new and second-hand leasing cars. Their smartphone-based access system ensures a hassle-free rental process and makes it easy for people to recuperate some of their monthly vehicle costs.

In the operator model, the company that runs the platform also owns the assets that are being rented out. Two notable examples are the bike-sharing service Mobike and electric scooter sharing service Bird. Both offer carbon-friendly transportation around town but also demonstrate that sharing services can have a downside. People don't take care of the vehicles as they would their own. Bikes and scooters are left in the middle of sidewalks and littered throughout parks. As a result, these shared vehicles' lifespan is much shorter than expected, raising questions about their environmental impact. Renting for short periods is also gaining traction in consumer electronics. Grover's subscription service offers rental access to over 2,000 tech products, including smartphones, laptops, VR gear, and wearables. After a specified time period, users return the tech, which is then rented out to the next user.

Rent Together

Bundling demand can help people save money, as described in Save Money (B9), but can also offer other benefits. For example, KoruKids developed a "family finder tool" to help close-by London families connect and share a nanny. When two families share a nanny, they save money, the nanny's wage increases, children find playmates, and KoruKids earns a commission, a quadruple win.

The use of a product in exchange for money can be described by two models: peer-to-peer and operator-driven

CIRCULAR ECONOMY

Two centuries ago, the industrial revolution changed the way we use – and sometimes abuse – our resources. Only now are we realizing that such massive use of resources is unsustainable. Recently, the world has begun looking for ways to conserve natural resources, minimize waste and pollution, lower emissions, and fairly distribute wealth. There is growing support across society to move from the unsustainable linear model, in which we take-make-waste resources, to a circular model, in which we design, make, and use things within the boundaries of our ecological and societal worlds.

The circular economy is a philosophy aimed at redefining growth. It decouples economic activity from the consumption of finite resources. It has three founding principles: removing waste and pollution from the system, keeping products and materials in use, and regenerating natural systems. Achieving a circular economy is a massive challenge that requires a shift from product-centric design to transformational system-based design.

The Ellen MacArthur Foundation is one of the driving forces behind the circular economy movement. Their circular economy system diagram illustrates a continuous flow of technical and biological materials through "value circles," described on the right page. The closer the loop sits to the center of the diagram, the more valuable the approach, e.g., prolonging the product's first life is most valuable, followed by reusing, refurbishing, and finally, recycling.

While the circular economy is driven by a systems perspective, this book takes a consumer benefit perspective. As a result, the design strategies in this book are structured differently than the value circles.

Right page: Ellen MacArthur Foundation, Circular economy systems diagram (February 2019)

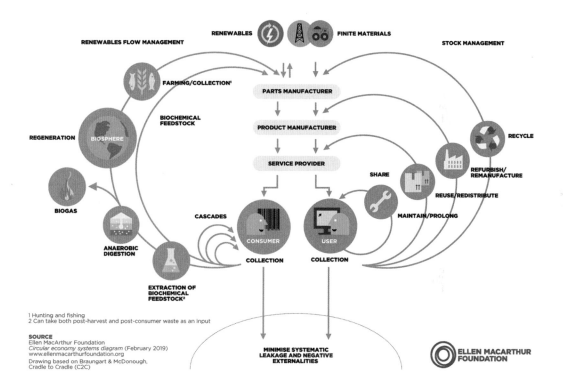

RENEWABLES FLOW MANAGEMENT

RENEWABLES

FINITE MATERIALS

STOCK MANAGEMENT

FARMING/COLLECTION[1]

PARTS MANUFACTURER

BIOCHEMICAL FEEDSTOCK

REGENERATION

BIOSPHERE

PRODUCT MANUFACTURER

RECYCLE

SERVICE PROVIDER

REFURBISH/ REMANUFACTURE

SHARE

BIOGAS

REUSE/REDISTRIBUTE

CASCADES

CONSUMER

USER

MAINTAIN/PROLONG

ANAEROBIC DIGESTION

COLLECTION

COLLECTION

EXTRACTION OF BIOCHEMICAL FEEDSTOCK[2]

1 Hunting and fishing
2 Can take both post-harvest and post-consumer waste as an input

MINIMISE SYSTEMATIC LEAKAGE AND NEGATIVE EXTERNALITIES

SOURCE
Ellen MacArthur Foundation
Circular economy systems diagram (February 2019)
www.ellenmacarthurfoundation.org
Drawing based on Braungart & McDonough,
Cradle to Cradle (C2C)

ELLEN MACARTHUR FOUNDATION

B22 LENGTHEN LIFESPAN

❝ The most sustainable gadget on the market is the one you already own[33]. ❞

Greenpeace

Consumers often discard tech products long before their end of life. This can be due to poor performance when the product gets slow or the battery life diminishes. It can also be due to the release of newer versions that offer more desirable features; seductive marketing often makes us buy products we don't really need. Just look at smartphones, which sell like hotcakes to novelty-seeking, fashion-conscious consumers. Keeping a mobile phone in use for only one extra year cuts its lifetime CO_2 impact by a third[34], as 80% of the greenhouse gasses for which a smartphone is responsible come from production[33].

Encouraging people to lengthen the use of their products should be done by combining different design strategy tactics. For example, if people can't update the software on their phone or install certain apps, they will soon replace it with a newer version, even if the phone is made of durable materials. Research from TU Delft[35] sustainability experts has helped to identify the following tactics for achieving longevity:

Design to Update

To maintain security, internet-connected products need regular updates. For manufacturers, this can be a nuisance. When Sonos announced in early 2020 that they would discontinue software updates for products manufactured before 2015, massive consumer blowback ensued online. Some even called for a boycott. In response, Sonos quickly announced that older products will continue to receive security patches, allowing consumers to safely use their old speakers. But they won't get access to new features.

Design to Upgrade

Technological developments quickly render today's products obsolete. For example, new applications and software slow down older smartphones lacking necessary processing power. Fairphone, the most sustainable smartphone on the market[33], is addressing fast obsoletion. Their modular design allows you to upgrade your smartphone's camera to a better version.

Design to Repair

In 2017, Greenpeace and iFixit, a global online repair community aimed at DIY repairs, assessed over 40 of the world's best-selling gadgets on repairability. In almost 70% of products assessed, they found it difficult to replace parts that commonly fail, such as the battery or display. iFixit aims to motivate manufacturers to make their products more repairable by publishing Smartphone Repairability Scores. In addition, iFixit makes DIY repair possible by creating manuals that describe how to repair products and selling the spare parts and tools needed to do so.

Design to Maintain

In the past, regular time intervals dictated when maintenance was done, regardless of how frequently products were used. Cars were brought in for annual maintenance. More recently, technology-enabled usage-based maintenance, which alerts drivers when it is time to bring in their car for maintenance, has become more widespread. Now, we're moving into the era of predictive maintenance, as technology can actively determine components' conditions and predict when care is needed. Tesla has already implemented this in their cars; if the vehicle's computer signals that a component needs replacing, it will order the part and let the driver know. As products become smarter and more connected, we hope to see predictive maintenance of washing machines, vacuum cleaners, coffee makers, and many more products in the future.

Design to Last

Choice of materials and the design of moving parts have a significant impact on product lifespan. Design for product durability aims to lengthen the product's functional value by designing robust products. Nokia phones were famous for their durability. No matter how often you dropped them or how poorly you cared for them, they always worked. Some people still use them today, a decade later. In contrast, the Samsung Galaxy 8 is one of the most breakable phones of all time due to edge-to-edge glass on both the front and back[36].

Nokia 3310

Design to Protect

We carry an increasing number of products with us, and as we become habituated to them, treating them carefully gets difficult. Dropping our phone is an all-too-common event. Twenty years ago, people who put cases on their durable Nokia phones were laughed at. Today, it is common sense to protect your smartphone, with cases even becoming fashion statements. Many of these cases make tech products feel a bit "less techy" as the use of natural materials gives them a "warm feel." Protective measures can also be digital. If smartphones get too hot, they may temporarily disable features like the camera flash or reduce processing power until they reach an acceptable temperature, or they may even shut down completely. If you're making a phone call on a hot summer day with your iPhone exposed to sunlight, you may experience an abrupt end to your call, followed by the message "iPhone needs to cool down before you can use it." Unlike computers, smartphones don't have built-in fans, relying instead on passive cooling methods and digital safety measures to prevent damage.

Design to Love

When people feel emotionally attached to a product, they tend to hold on to it. Product aesthetics can help people form these attachments. Emotional bonding can also be stimulated through Personalize (B2), for example. Bang & Olufsen, a luxury consumer electronics brand, excels at designing for longevity, and people tend to take pride in their products. For example, the Beosound Shape is a modular speaker concept that becomes a piece of art on your wall. You can set the size, shape, color, and even sound performance to your liking. Each tile functions as a speaker, amplifier, or acoustic damper. The tiles can be arranged, rearranged, or expanded, and system colors can be changed.

Design to Reuse

Products can be directly reused, like smartphones passed on to family and friends, given to charity, or sold to strangers on eBay. However, reuse can also mean redefining a product's purpose. For instance, a laptop that is getting too slow for office work could be repurposed as a great media server, file server, or image library. An old smartphone could become a picture frame for digital art. All these products need are the right accessories and special software, and a few tweaks can prevent them from ending up in a landfill. Tech product manufacturers are not seizing this opportunity yet.

Encouraging people
to lengthen the use
of their products
should be done by
combining different
design strategy
tactics

Bang & Olufsen Beosound Shape

B23 REDUCE FOOTPRINT

Growing awareness of our lifestyle choices' effect on climate change and our planet's diminishing resources increases consumer interest in products and companies with a low environmental footprint. While design strategies like Increase Efficiency (B10), Facilitate Sharing (B21), and Lengthen Lifespan (B22) can all help reduce your product's footprint, they focus on other key benefits. Reduce Footprint is a complementary design strategy. It establishes a product's low environmental footprint as a consumer benefit through the following seven tactics:

Offer Your Product as a Service

Instead of just selling a sustainable product, offering it as a service will help you maintain control over its environmental footprint. Gerrard Street, for example, offers subscription-based, high-quality headphones. Driven by their mission to reduce electronic waste, Gerrard Street's headphones can be easily disassembled, repaired, refurbished, or upgraded due to their modular design.

Include Eco-Friendly Choices

As described in Increase Efficiency (B10), product efficiency should always be a key point for reducing your product's footprint. However, products that sacrifice performance for decreased energy consumption may be less attractive to consumers. Adding an optional eco-friendly operation mode can be a good solution. Washing machines offer eco-wash programs that consume less energy but take longer to complete. Cars offer eco modes that improve fuel efficiency but affect acceleration, creating a different driving experience.

As is common with airplane ticket purchases, offering consumers the option to offset their individual carbon footprints is worth considering. Apps like Capture Club use GPS tracking to calculate your trip's carbon footprint and offset it with a single click. Mobility providers wishing to position themselves as sustainable alternatives could integrate this feature into their products.

Sell Good-as-New Used Products

While the purchase of secondhand cars, furniture, or clothing is typical, most people prefer buying brand new tech products. Luckily, price and sustainability concerns have caused a growing number of consumers to show interest in high-quality secondhand electronics. Samsung offers 'Certified pre-owned phones' that have been taken apart, inspected, and partially replaced if necessary. After reassembly, the phones get a software update and undergo 400 rigorous tests to ensure their condition. The phones are then shipped with a new charger, a fresh set of headphones, and a one-year warranty. Third-party refurbishment companies and independent marketplaces like Back Market help companies who don't want to create their own refurbishment program.

Engage in Recycling

We see countless examples of tech products that are impossible to recycle due to design choices: batteries glued to the product casing, materials mixed with toxic chemicals, and so on. Making your products easy to recycle requires special attention in the design process.

Running your own recycling program will make it easy for consumers to recycle their products and increase recycling rates. Apple's trade-in program accepts smartphones, tablets, computers, watches, drives, mice, keyboards, printers, iPods, and more. In some cases, Apple will exchange Apple Store credit for the device. Apple isn't the only one encouraging electronics recycling; companies like LG, Samsung, Sony, and Xerox all offer mail-in or drop-off stations for their products. Be aware that recycling should be a last resort; design strategies like Lengthen Lifespan (B22) and tactics like "Selling Good-as-New Used Products" are far better for the environment.

Another way to engage in recycling is incorporating recycled materials into your new tech products. Sony developed SORPLASTM, a recycled plastic that offers both sustainability and high performance for use in their consumer products. SORPLASTM will enable Sony to manufacture products with up to 99% recycled plastics without any performance loss.

Go Carbon-Negative

Consumers are expanding their concern for environmental impact beyond the product; companies' overall carbon profiles are becoming more important to consumers. After all, buying from carbon-neutral companies is an easy way for consumers to lower their own footprint. Many big tech companies have begun announcing serious commitments. Microsoft, for example, promises to be carbon negative by 2030. Search engine Ecosia is already carbon negative, producing its own solar electricity and using its profits to plant trees. They claim that every search request removes 1kg of CO_2 from the atmosphere.

Create Environmentally Friendly Side Effects

While reducing your product's environmental footprint is great, adding a positive effect from use is even better. Hydrogen cars claim a lower environmental footprint than combustion engine cars. But there's more: Hyundai claims that driving their NEXO hydrogen car actually cleans the air instead of polluting it like conventional cars do. The car filters harmful particles out of the air and only exhausts water vapor. While driving, the car creates enough clean air for 42 people at once.

Offer Transparency

Being transparent about your product's footprint can help environment-conscious consumers make better purchasing decisions. Carbon footprint labeling is an excellent way to offer transparency. As fast-moving consumer goods pave the way, tech products closely follow. Most footprint labels will depict "cradle-to-grave" carbon footprints, measuring the product's total greenhouse gas emissions, from the extraction of raw materials to the product's manufacture, distribution, use, and eventual disposal[37].

B24 UNLEASH NEW VALUE

While providing new functionality is not the quickest route to success, getting it right could be your claim to fame. The key to developing new functionality is deep consumer insight.

People can't always express what they want or need. However, needs hidden deep down can be discovered through observation and probing. Innovators should be able to connect the dots and see hidden opportunities.

New functionality can either be framed as a new product feature or based on an entirely new value proposition.

Offer a New Feature

Enhancing the user experience can be done by adding a new feature to an existing product. 'Dog mode,' a climate control feature implemented by Tesla, runs the car's air conditioning or heater when owners leave their pets in the vehicle. This offers dog owners mobility, as they can leave their dog safely in the car as they run errands or go for lunch.

It's important to realize that people can have difficulty envisioning a feature's value when technology is immature. When the first camera phone was sold 20 years ago, people did not see the value. Who needs a low-quality camera integrated into a bulky phone? At this time, phone manufacturers were in a race to deliver the smallest phones possible, and social media didn't exist yet. Nowadays, the idea of a mobile phone without a camera seems absurd; almost nobody would buy a phone without one. The number of cameras has even become a performance metric, with some smartphones boasting up to 5 cameras.

Offer a New Value Proposition

New value propositions can arise from a combination of features that unlock new uses. For example, the combination of smart locks, location tracking, and an app-based reservation and payment system enabled a new bike-sharing value proposition.

As the name states, a new value proposition is predicated upon bringing new value to people. This means that the underlying product features don't have to be new to the world. When Steve Jobs first revealed the iPad in 2010, tablet computers had already been around for a while. Yet, Jobs introduced the iPad as a product that "creates and defines an entirely new category of devices." The value proposition of a powerful device with a full browser controlled by your fingers, enabling you to hold the internet in your hands, made it the first tablet to go mainstream. The iPad hit the innovation sweet spot, offering certain computer functionalities in a completely new format, with an interface suitable for users of all ages. Over time, the iPad has even developed into a powerful tool for businessmen.

People can't always express what they want or need.

iPad

❝ iPad creates and defines an entirely new category of devices that will connect users with their apps and content in a much more intimate, intuitive and fun way than ever before. ❞

Steve Jobs

○ Rhetoric is key. If people are unaware of their own needs, they won't understand why they need your new product or feature. Talk about benefits and value, not features!

○ Take an iterative approach: test and improve your idea and message multiple times before bringing it to market. The devil's in the details.

○ Don't just listen to what people say; go observe what people DO. The key to discovering latent needs is observation.

○ Don't expect an easy ride; the road to success might be bumpier and longer than expected. You will need to educate the market, which requires significant marketing efforts. Hang in there!

SMART GLASSES

Case Study

When first attempting to develop revolutionary consumer tech products, innovators often fail to hit the innovation sweet spot. Either products are too expensive, benefits too weak, or consumer expectations not met. Companies quickly remove these products from the market and "pivot," shifting their product or business strategy. The following are two examples of products that haven't worked out as planned.

Google Glass

Google Glass was a revolutionary new product. Taking the form of eyeglasses, Glass was a miniature, head-mounted, voice-controlled smartphone. It projected a heads-up display onto a tiny piece of glass within the wearer's field of vision, visible only to them. Glass could even capture video and still images.

Google was excellent at creating hype around the product. They first released their beta version to the small "Glass Explorers" community, who could buy Google Glass for $1,500 beginning in April 2013, over a year before the product became available to the public.

Google left Glass's possibilities open to the imagination of the community and the wider public, who assumed that Google Glass would be worn in public. People became wary of being unwittingly filmed, causing massive opposition to the product. They feared that Glass, coupled with

facial recognition software, could allow them to be identified in public (lack of Preserve Data Privacy, R2). The media picked up on this, and it wasn't long before most people viewed Google Glass as a means to violate privacy laws and named Google Glass users "Glassholes" (lack of Fit Social Norms, R10).

Combined with a lack of clear functional benefits, Google Glass's negative social connotations doomed it to failure. In January 2015, Google announced that it would stop producing the Google Glass Explorer edition. Mid 2017 saw Google announce the Glass Enterprise Edition, targeting the workplace instead of the home. They described it as "a small, lightweight wearable computer with a transparent display for hands-free work". Google targets workers that need both hands, highlighting use cases in manufacturing, logistics, and healthcare (Design for Marketing Strategies, R13).

Magic Leap

Magic Leap is one of the most hyped startups of the last decade. Founded in 2010, they raised $3 billion from Google, the Alibaba Group, and 25 other investors to develop their mixed-reality goggles. Their revolutionary product would project realistic 3D computer-generated imagery over real-world objects. By using exclusive demos, the highly secretive startup impressed investors and influential journalists, prompting magazines like Wired to write laudatory articles. As the hype increased, everybody thought Magic Leap would become "the next Apple."

Launched at the end of 2018, Magic Leap's first product looked like goggles out of a science fiction movie. By belt-mounting most of the electronics in a pocket-sized computer, they made their goggles light and comfortable. Attempting to define a brand-new product category, Magic Leap stressed that their product is a spatial computer, not VR or a smartphone AR. Regardless, the goggles didn't sell well. They promised Performance (B11) and New Value (B24) but couldn't deliver on the expectations they had created. At $2295, the gadget's costs far outweighed its practical value.

In early 2020, Magic Leap ran out of money, fired 1,000 people, and replaced its founder CEO. They pivoted, raising additional funding and narrowing their focus to professional applications. In collaboration with strategic partners, they now target business use cases like virtual teamwork for remote office workers, worker training and assistance, and collaborative work on designs, 3D models, and data (Build Partnerships R9 and Design for Marketing Strategies R13). Whether Magic Leap can successfully compete with the much cheaper Google Glass ($999) and the well-established, well-performing Microsoft HoloLens ($3,500) has yet to be seen.

Wearable technology, including smart glasses like Magic Leap and Google Glass, is just getting started. It is gaining traction in business applications where the benefits are apparent and the social tension it causes is low. In a few years, when prices drop as the technology advances, they are likely to reappear in consumer markets.

TO DESIGN TECH PRODUCTS THAT MAKE SENSE, YOU NEED TO STRENGTHEN PRODUCT BENEFITS AND MITIGATE CONSUMER RESISTANCE

MITIGATE

RESISTANCE

13 Design Strategies to
MITIGATE RESISTANCE

Tech products often encounter some form of resistance from consumers. New tech products have yet to prove themselves, might cause unintended side effects, or might quickly become outdated. As a result, consumers may fear the risks associated with their purchase and use.

Most resistance can be traced back to perceptions of different risk types[38] involved in buying or using a product: *physical risks*, in case a product harms our health, our possessions, or our environment; *operational risks*, in case a product doesn't perform or is unreliable; *economic risks*, in case the product offers low value for money, needs repairs, or breaks down completely; *risks of time-loss*, in which case consumers invest time and effort without satisfactory results. Other, less tangible risks include *social risks*, in case others disapprove of the product and their users, and *psychological risks*, in case the product doesn't fit a person's values or self-image.

To successfully mitigate resistance through your product's design, you'll need a deep understanding of consumers' values, belief structures, needs, risk perceptions, and their expectations of your product's potential drawbacks. Engaging with consumers throughout the innovation process will shed light on how your product may negatively affect consumers' lives, society, and our planet.

Mitigating resistance is not about persuading consumers to adopt your product; it is about developing better products that trigger less resistance simply because consumers have less to be concerned about. The extent to which you foresee and address possible resistance in your product's design will affect your product's speed of adoption and overall success. The design strategies in this section of the book will help you identify such resistance. You will find that the design strategies to mitigate resistance become increasingly powerful when applied in combination with each other.

Understanding resistance will help you develop better products that trigger less resistance

R1 INCREASE PERSONAL SAFETY

For centuries, people have been afraid that new technologies and innovations would cause them harm. In 1865, the UK enacted the "Red Flag Act," limiting motor vehicle speed to 5 kilometers per hour. The act even required a man to walk in front of all motor vehicles while holding a red flag to warn pedestrians of the approaching car. Today, some people label self-driving cars as racist killing machines due to algorithms that ineffectively recognize all skin types and raise the potential for fatal accidents. Our concerns are not just about physical safety; the mentally addictive effects of social media and games are the talk of the day. The following tactics can reduce people's fear of physical or mental harm:

Include Automated Safety Interventions

If the product features the ability to help keep you safe, it should do just that. Therefore, some innovations ship with built-in precautionary measures. For example, automated safety features like an Anti-lock Braking System (ABS) are now standard safety features in all modern cars. ABS prevents your wheels from locking up when the brakes engage and restores traction to your tires. Today it is a mandatory feature for all new cars. Soon, automated safety features will be implemented into speed pedelecs: a new category of electric bikes on the rise in Europe allows cyclists to travel up to 45 kmph. Dutch lawmakers are now discussing integrating GPS-enabled speed regulators, designed to automatically restrict pedelec speed within designated, high traffic areas. In partnership with the Delft University of Technology, the bicycle company Gazelle is developing smart steering assistance aimed at reducing falls on electric bicycles. The smart motor in the handlebars corrects steering if you're at risk of falling.

> Our concerns are not just about physical safety; the mentally addictive effects of social media and games are the talk of the day

Include Not-to-Be-Missed Safety Alerts

Human errors are a significant cause of traffic accidents. While self-driving cars promise a future with fewer accidents, the technology today is far from perfect. Tesla's autopilot mode continuously evaluates its own capability in any given situation. If it thinks it won't be able to safely handle a situation, it alerts the driver to "Take Over Immediately" with unmissable flashing lights and very loud beeps. To ensure that drivers remain alert and awake, Subaru implements cameras and infrared sensors to monitor eye movements for distractions. If they detect you falling asleep behind the wheel or disregarding the road, the car sounds an alarm.

Include Desirable Safety Accessories

Fear of everyday products and services dissuade many people from using them. Some people are afraid of being injured in accidents when riding a bike, with electric bikes only enhancing these fears. While their greater speed allows you to travel much faster, it also increases the risk of personal harm. Manufacturers of electric bikes would be wise to include helmets with the sale of their bikes to address people's fear of accidents. However, most people don't like helmets; they look silly and ruin hairdos. Hövding, a Swedish safety company, addressed this problem by developing an airbag for cyclists. The airbag sits stylishly around your neck, nearly unnoticeable, deploying only in case of an emergency. As Hövding puts it, "the world's safest bicycle helmet isn't a helmet." Enabled by sensors and algorithms, their product allows people to feel safer while cycling at high speeds, without the hassle of a helmet.

While Hövding makes the helmet invisible, Livall chose another route to make safety cool. Their helmet's high-tech appearance makes it the perfect product for tech-savvy consumers. The Livall Commuter is packed with smart safety features. It has a remote control attached to the handlebar that allows you to trigger the helmet's turn signals, play music, and answer calls. It reads you GPS directions and offers 270° visibility lights for your night commute. The helmet also alerts a preset safety contact in case its 3-axis gyroscope detects a fall. Combined, the features packed into the Livall helmet remove any reason to take your hands off the handlebars, reducing the chance of an accident.

Hövding helmet

Include Self-Protection

While built-in safety measures increase overall safety and can overcome people's reluctance to use the product, they tend to make some people complacent. Some people take self-driving mode as an invitation to ignore the road completely, however, self-driving isn't perfect yet; drivers need to keep watching the road. In response to this, Tesla made it mandatory to have at least one hand on the wheel while in self-driving mode. Sensors in the steering wheel detect when light pressure is applied. If nothing is detected for some time, the

While built-in safety measures increase overall safety and can overcome people's reluctance to use the product, they tend to make some people complacent

car prompts the driver to "apply light pressure to the steering wheel." It grabs your attention by use of blinking lights and increasingly frequent beeps until you comply.

Samsung's In-Traffic Reply app automatically replies to messages you receive while driving. The app uses your phone's sensors to detect when you're driving or biking and automatically activates. While on the move, it responds to incoming messages with fun, preset replies, informing people you're unavailable until you arrive.

Social media can be addictive; people are rewarded with dopamine shots when they check their feeds. Coinciding with the finalization of this book, a new social network trying a different approach launched. Sundayy is removing the addictive effects from social media while still allowing you to stay up to date on friends' lives. Instead of accumulating likes and friends, the network's goal is to stay in touch with a close group of friends and family members. It saves your daily reflections Monday through Saturday, and shares these once a week with your connections, on Sunday.

Include Restrictive Measures

Some products meet consumer resistance because people fear their daily use may cause harm to them or others. Quooker developed a 3-in-1 kitchen tap, dispensing cold, hot, and boiling water. They realized that boiling water straight from the tap may worry parents and addressed this concern in the product's design. Quooker's complex press-turn activation movement is child-proof. Also, the boiling water flow is made up of fine drops instead of a solid jet, reducing the chances of severe burns. On top of that, Quooker points out that taps, unlike kettles, cannot tip over, highlighting that their product is safer than a traditional kettle.

Include Off-line Usage

Some people hesitate to use wearables, as they fear the EMF radiation emitted from these devices can have unhealthy side-effects. Oura is a wearables company that developed a pulse-measuring ring. They use this data to score you on readiness, sleep, and activity. Oura explicitly states that the ring is EMF safe and allows users to activate airplane mode without losing any of the ring's functionalities. When Airplane Mode is enabled, the ring doesn't send or receive any signals but does continue to collect data for up to six weeks. When to connect in order to upload data to your smartphone is up to you.

Include User Verification and Reviews

Certain platforms enable us to get in touch with people we have never met before, from the people we date to those who crash on our couch. Identity verification can increase people's peace of mind when using these products. CouchSurfing is a platform that connects people who need somewhere to sleep with people willing to share their couch. Understandably, users of the platform expect a thorough identity verification process before they let a stranger sleep on their couch. CouchSurfing's optional verification process allows people to verify their ID, phone number, and address. To persuade users to get verified, verification comes with free access to the newest features and priority support. Also, other users of the platform can see whether you have completed the identity check. The process is app-based and only takes minutes to complete. First, the CouchSurfing app will ask you to take a photo of a government-issued identity card, like a passport, driver's license, or ID card. It will also ask you to take a photo of your face using your mobile phone's camera. The photo is then automatically compared to the photo on your ID card to confirm that the card belongs to you. In addition, CouchSurfing offers user-generated reviews and a variety of safety tips. Coupled with a little common sense, CouchSurfing users can breathe easy, being reasonably certain that the person on their couch is legitimate.

DOS & DON'TS

○ While people's fears of physical or mental harm may not be grounded, they are real. Take them seriously and address them in your design.

○ Look for opportunities to include safety features in your product and add them as separate accessories or add-ons.

○ Don't make your products addictive. When it comes to digital products, people are increasingly looking for easy protection from themselves.

○ Don't underestimate human behavior. As soon as people become accustomed to and get too comfortable with safety features, they may adapt their behavior in such a way that the features are no longer effective. For example, people have been caught sleeping in their car while driving on autopilot.

R2 PRESERVE DATA PRIVACY

The meteoric rise of digital technologies has brought along its fair share of concerns. Tech giants have our data to thank for their growth. They collect data from our interactions with their platforms to create profiles of us. The enormous scale of data collection has caused unease, with people growing distrustful of the platforms they use. The following tactics can help alleviate privacy concerns:

Collect Less Data

The most straightforward way to give consumers peace of mind is to keep as little data as possible. DuckDuckGo is a search engine whose main appeal is its one-sentence data collection policy. "We don't collect or share personal information." As a result, DuckDuckGo has become the default search engine for people who don't want their personal info stored online and are fed up with being profiled.

Make Data Private

Some companies make their product so secure that it is (almost) impossible, even for themselves, to tap into user-generated data. This is how messaging app Signal made security their differentiator over competing solutions. Their state-of-the-art end-to-end encryption keeps your conversations secure. Not even Signal can eavesdrop on you, as communication encryption keys are generated and stored on your smartphone. The Signal Protocol is fully open source, and its development and maintenance are funded by a non-profit: the Signal Technology Foundation. In February 2020, the European Commission recommended their employees use Signal for external communication[39].

> **❝ I use Signal every day. #notesforFBI (Spoiler: they already know)[40]❞**
> Edward Snowden on Twitter

Offer Control over Data Sharing

Nowadays, many people feel like they have no control over who can access their data. In this regard, Apple's reputation is better than most other big tech companies, due not only to how they treat people's data but also to the level of control they give to people over who can access their data. Apple Health collects heaps of data on your body and activity, especially if you use an Apple Watch. In their app, you can decide which health data your other apps can access. For example, the Nike Run Club app can only read or write data with your permission. You can set individual permissions for specific data items, like active energy, heart rate, walking and running distance, and workouts.

Give People Data Ownership

Non-profit organizations and privacy advocates are working on new concepts to give people ownership over their data. Sir Tim Berners-Lee, one of the inventors of the internet, realized that his original vision for the World Wide Web never materialized. Solid is his second attempt at achieving his vision of a secure, decentralized exchange of public and private data. Solid rents out personal web servers for your data called Pods, keeping your data secure and easily accessible. You retain complete ownership and control over the data in your pods, where each pod is stored, what data each pod contains, and which applications can use which parts of your data. You can share slices of your data with the people, organizations, and applications of your choosing and can revoke that access at any time.

Enable Data Deletion

Erasing data can be done on both a company level and a product level. European citizens have the power to demand that any company erase all data the company holds on them, as specified in the GDPR's "right to be forgotten." On a product level, erasing data is not (yet) regulated. This raises an interesting question: can you actually delete all of your personal data when you sell your product for reuse or bring it to a recycling center? Apple has made this very simple with their "restore to factory settings" function. A few clicks are all it takes to permanently erase all your info from your iPhone.

DOS & DON'TS

O Keep privacy in mind when designing your tech product. Make it a goal, not an afterthought.

O Be transparent about data use. Communicate to people what you're using their data for.

O Don't hide things. If you had a security breach, proactively communicate what happened, what measures you took, and what was or is currently exposed.

O Don't ignore or fail to inform yourself about local regulations. They can vary per country.

(LOSS OF) PRIVACY

The last few decades witnessed the explosive growth of digital technologies. Facebook, founded in 2004, is now worth 778 billion dollars. Google recently became the fourth company ever to surpass a one trillion-dollar evaluation, joining Apple, Amazon, and Microsoft in the tech juggernauts' highest echelon.

The monumental success of these companies is mainly due to one thing: our data. Apple's famously simple user interface has been perfected by user experience data. No stranger to data collection, Facebook compiles all of your personal data to build a detailed profile of you, predicting your age, sex, emotional stability, intelligence, religion, relationship status, and much more.[41] They use this profile to sell advertisers access to you. In 2019, Facebook pulled in a revenue of 70 billion dollars, over 98% coming from advertising[42].

Unsurprisingly, American companies are taking the lead in commercializing our data, as the US and Europe have very different approaches to data and privacy regulation. The US regards data as a commercial asset owned by corporations, governed by state-level legislation, and supervised by the Federal Trade Commission. Europe, on the other hand, prioritizes individual rights over business interests. Privacy and data protection are defined as fundamental freedoms under the European Union Charter, and companies are held liable if they violate Europe's strict GDPR requirements.

As big tech grows, big data grows with it. The unprecedented level of data collection occurring today has raised a lot of concern. To address this, some privacy measures have been put into place. For example, websites ask you to agree to long and complicated terms and conditions before use. However, these measures are far from adequate. A 2016 survey[43] found that 74% of people accepted privacy policies without even reading them. People accept the privacy policies for access to the website, not because they trust it.

Julia Janssen, a Dutch artist who creates awareness of the impact of digitalization on society, launched her project "0.0146 seconds" in 2019[44]. She demonstrates that in just one click, 0.0146 seconds, you might accept 835 privacy policies that would take hundreds of hours to read. She indicates that by accepting the privacy policy of www.dailymail.co.uk, you're not only accepting the online newspaper's privacy policy but also the 834 privacy policies of its partners. All legal, as it complies with the "informed consent" guidelines for collecting our data.

More and more companies are shifting from a design with privacy as an afterthought to a design that prioritizes privacy. Privacy by Design is an increasingly popular framework used to embed privacy into the design and operation of digital systems and business practices. For more information on Privacy by Design, visit: https://en.wikipedia.org/wiki/Privacy_by_design

PRIVACY BY DESIGN IS BASED ON SEVEN "FOUNDATIONAL PRINCIPLES:"

1. Proactive not reactive; preventive, not remedial
2. Privacy as the default setting
3. Privacy embedded into design
4. Full functionality – positive-sum, not zero-sum
5. End-to-end security – full lifecycle protection
6. Visibility and transparency – keep it open
7. Respect for user privacy – keep it user-centric

CANDLE

Candle, "the privacy-friendly smart home," demonstrates that smart home solutions can feature both privacy and convenience. Led by Tijmen Schep, a team of independent Dutch designers and privacy experts started Candle as a research project. They proved that you can create easy-to-use smart home solutions that keep all your data within your home.

Candle is particularly interesting because of its dual privacy focus. They keep everything that happens in the home private from the outside world while also maintaining privacy within family life's social dynamics. The sensors throughout smart homes can significantly impact children's lives by making it far more difficult to keep secrets from parents. For example, since CO_2 levels rise as room occupancy increases, CO_2 sensors can tell how many people were in a room. Smart locks reveal when which people come and go. Smart light switches log when lights are turned on and off. No more secretly bringing a date or friends over. No more sneaking in and out of the home. No more lights on after bedtime. Growing up in a smart home can cause children to feel like they're always being monitored.

Candle believes that "smart devices should be able to tell little white lies once in a while." They back this up by allowing users to delete, manipulate or even create data points in their data logs. Some Candle devices can even generate fake data, bending the truth by temporarily stabilizing CO_2 levels or omitting smart lock data.

Included in the Candle system is a smart thermostat, sensors to measure humidity, carbon, and fine dust, an electricity use sensor, a smart lock, a weather station, and a smart alarm clock that can gradually brighten the lights in your bedroom. Their plant health sensor even checks if your plants are thirsty. Either use your smartphone, voice, or laptop to control devices or turn them on or off using their physical switches.

Today, Candle is not a commercial product. Their team encourages people to build their own smart home and provide manuals and documentation to make this as easy as possible. They explain which components you need and how to put them together, claiming anybody can build a smart device in half an hour and an entire smart home system in a day. While Candle's products mostly attract privacy-aware and tech-savvy consumers, they don't require any programming or soldering skills.

R2 PRESERVE DATA PRIVACY

Candle is 100% privacy friendly; it never communicates with any external server. No data leaves your home; it is stored in your smart home hub. Even voice control is entirely cloudless.

R5 GIVE CONTROL

Users can manipulate their data logs by deleting, changing, or inserting any data point. Some devices have a "generate fake data" button, enabling you, for example, to pretend you are alone in a room. On-off switches and the ability to unplug USB microphones give users physical control over their device.

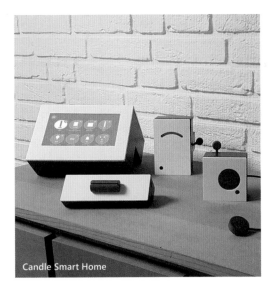

Candle Smart Home

R3 OFFER TRANSPARENCY

All code is open source and available to everybody on GitHub.

R4 Boost Security

Candle's devices are not connected to the internet, decreasing their vulnerability to security breaches and hacks. One device offers additional protection by allowing you to disconnect your home from the internet when you're asleep or away.

B22 Lengthen Lifespan

Modular designs are easily upgradeable if better modules become available. In addition, the absence of third-party services means there is no risk of service providers going out of business and rendering your devices useless.

B6 Enable Anytime, Anywhere

Due to the "build-your-own" nature of the service, you can add or combine features to the devices in your home as you like. Alternatively, you can choose to make them stand-alone devices, showing only limited data on their screens. If you do connect them to a local controller, you can graph and keep track of your data over time.

R3 OFFER TRANSPARENCY

Trust goes hand-in-hand with transparency, which is about much more than data. These days, we expect companies to be transparent about how they make money, how they source products, and anything else they do that might affect our lives or the environment. The following tactics can help to build trust through transparency:

Join the "Open Movement"

The open movement is all about transparency, free access, collaboration, and re-use. It encompasses many sub-movements like open source, open data, open government, and open science. Open source and open data are most relevant for tech product design. GitHub, a repository hosting service at the core of the open-source movement, allows innovation teams to store and share their project's files and data. If you choose to make them publicly available, anybody can inspect them. It's like Google Drive for tech products. Some well-known open source products include the Linux operating system and Arduino electronics.

Innovators who embrace open source must immediately consider which license is best for their project, as it can influence their innovation process and business model. There are dozens of different open source licenses. If this topic is new to you, visit https://choosealicense.com; this Github-curated website offers an easy starting point.

Open data and public data are open datasets, free for anyone to access, use, reuse, and/or redistribute. Tech communities are now creating open datasets curated as a resource to offer transparency on training data and reduce bias in algorithms. Microsoft used such datasets to develop their Video Authenticator, a tool that gives "a confidence score, or percentage chance" that media has been manipulated. The tool was created using a public dataset from Face Forensic++ and was tested on the DeepFake Detection Challenge Dataset. Both are established datasets for training and testing deepfake detection technologies.

Be Open About Data and Algorithms

People can be hesitant to use algorithm-based products or share their data if they're unclear about what data and which algorithms are being used. The city of Amsterdam is a frontrunner in offering transparency to its citizens. Among other things, the Algorithm Register they are building explains which algorithms, AI systems, and data they use. They invite everyone to participate in building Amsterdam's human-centered AI by giving feedback.

While algorithms often run in the background, we are only confronted with their outcomes. For example, social media and news platforms use algorithms to detect fake news. If the algorithm-calculated probability score is above a certain threshold, the post is removed. Media platforms could help contain fake news by displaying posts' "trustworthiness score," empowering people to better decide what to share.

Be Open About Future Plans

In anticipation of future product features, some companies decide to preemptively include the specific hardware needed to support these features. Initially inactive, future software updates will enable the hardware. In these cases, full transparency is critical. In 2019, Google announced that the hub of their home security system, the Nest Guard, would receive voice-activated Google Assistant functionality through a software update. This came as a shock to Nest Guard owners, who were unaware that it had a microphone in the first place. They felt lied to and were afraid that Google had been secretly listening in on their conversations.

Be Open About Corporate Practices

Corporate transparency is about making your company's actions observable to outsiders. It can be about anything: environmental impact, working conditions, wages, sourcing, business models, pricing mechanisms, strategic partnerships, company values, data and privacy policies, ethical guidelines, and much more. One of the reasons most companies are not fully transparent is their fear of losing their competitive edge. Another is that with observability, comes accountability. Not every company is ready to be held accountable for its actions.

DOS & DON'TS

O Be upfront with people about your data use. Tell them what you use, how you use it, and why you use it.

O Inform people about features you intend to implement down the road and how their current products are already equipped for this.

O Don't try to cover up a mistake. If something happens involving user data, inform them right away. Your honesty will pay off.

O Don't "keep consumers dumb." Share what you know and empower them to make decisions.

AI COMPANIES AND TRANSPARENCY

Special

The impact algorithms have on our lives and society as a whole is increasing. To ensure a fair, inclusive, sustainable world, we need transparent, explainable, and auditable algorithms. However, transparency should not be limited to algorithms; transparency should be considered in every aspect of AI companies and organizations. Communication should be universally understandable, regardless of people's AI or business knowledge.

These pages present you with an overview of things you can - and should - be transparent about. Although it might not be complete, addressing this list will likely make you the most transparent AI company on the planet.

Your Impact on Society

The intended results of your product and possible unintended side effects.

What your product can/can't be used for.

Whether you hire people in low-cost countries or through crowdsourcing platforms for collecting or labeling data, training or maintaining AI systems, or other such tasks.

What you do to ensure fair and healthy employment conditions for your own employees and the other people involved in the value chain.

Your Impact on Our Planet

How much energy you use in total, and per "consumer service unit" (e.g., a search query, a measurement, or advice).

What kind of energy you use (renewable/fossil), and how much of it you generate yourself.

What you do to reduce and/or compensate for CO_2 emissions and other environmental harms.

Your Business Model

How you make money (paid service, advertisements, data sales, etc.).

How revenue stream percentages compare to each other.

What are your legal entities, and how are they funded (investors, subsidies, sponsors, etc.).

Your Purpose and Ethical Framework

Why the company started; what you are trying to achieve.

The ethical guidelines everyone in the company must follow.

Your organization's governance structure to ensure an ethical business and responsible innovation.

The positive and potentially negative impact your product might have on individuals, society, and our planet.

Your Governance for Data and Algorithms

The risks of biases in your system, at launch and over time.

What measures you take to identify, prevent, and deal with bias, discrimination, etc.

What type of audits you do, how you share the results, and who performs the audits.

How you ensure your partners and suppliers adhere to your rules, regulations, and ethics.

To what extent you are working together with public stakeholders to ensure trustworthy, socially responsible outcomes (academic researchers, tech communities, privacy advocates, NGOs, etc.).

If and how you deal with feedback from users and other stakeholders.

Your Algorithms

What kind of algorithms you use, and why you chose these.

If and how you share source code.

If and which open source software you use.

What decisions are being made by algorithms.

If and how you share a confidence score for algorithms' outcomes.

How your algorithms work, and what are the most influential data variables.

How open your algorithms are, and to what extent you can reconstruct outcomes.

To what extent outcomes can be explained and ethically justified by a human.

What training and test data was used, how this was collected, and if/how you altered this data.

If and how you share training data sets.

How your algorithms were trained and tested, and how they are maintained.

If algorithms that users interact with are continuously learning or if you work with regular (certified) releases.

How and when you assess if your algorithms are fair and ethical.

How your algorithms perform compared to alternatives.

Your (Users') Data

What data you use and why you need it.

How, when, and where you collect which data.

If, why, and how you alter the data your collect.

How long you store which data.

Where the data is geographically stored.

Your Users' Rights

Who owns which data.

If and how you gain approval to collect and use personal data.

If, how, and when you inform people of their interaction with algorithms.

What decisions about users are made by algorithms.

If and how users can receive explanations of how decisions are made.

If and how users can dispute a decision that was made about them.

If and how users can opt out of data collection.

If and how users can control which data they share.

If and how users can get insight into everything you know about them.

If and how users can request to have some or all of their data removed.

If and how users can change the data you have on them.

If and how customers can ask for a human to make a decision instead of an algorithm.

Where the company is located, and which countries' laws apply.

How you keep users informed, for example, in case of changes in terms and conditions.

R4 MAKE IT SECURE

As our use of connected devices and online services increases, our data exposure and product vulnerability rapidly grow. Luckily, most people are becoming more aware of security's importance. Security should go beyond just computers and smartphones; we must also secure our smart TVs, doorbells, locks, coffee machines, and many other connected products. Often, these products were not designed with security as a key priority. Failure to secure them can leave our data exposed and give intruders a chance to hijack our home electronics. The following are four ways to enhance your product's security:

Make Security Modular

There is often a trade-off between security and convenience. Adopting a modular approach to security allows consumers to select the options that best fit their risk-taking profile. Tesla is an excellent example of this, allowing car owners to create the security level they desire. "Manual Entry" requires a key to enter, while "Passive Entry" unlocks the car whenever your smartphone or key fob is within range. You can enable "PIN to Drive," a two-factor authentication that requires you to enter a four-digit code before driving. "Sentry Mode" adds additional security; the car monitors suspicious activities around your Tesla when it's parked and locked. Finally, all models come equipped with a security alarm system that you can turn on and off, which is upgradeable for some models.

Make Security Biometric

In 2016, Samsung was the first to bring facial recognition to smartphones, with Apple right on their heels. One glance at your smartphone is all it takes to unlock it. It removed the hassle of pin codes and the finicky fingerprint unlock and persuaded many people to secure their phones. Facial recognition is also safer, as pin codes are nothing more than extremely weak passwords. However, while approving payments with just your face is extremely user friendly, it could lead to accidental purchases. Companies tackle this in differing ways, all seeking to strike the right balance between ease of use and security. Apple Pay requires you to look at your phone and double-press the lock button to verify your App store purchases. Alibaba's "Smile to Pay" is even easier: it requires you to look into the camera and smile to approve a purchase.

Make Security Updates Attractive

Products' digital elements are vulnerable to being hacked. Vulnerabilities are found, exploited, and patched in a non-stop fight between hackers and developers. These constant changes necessitate continual software updates to maintain product security. Companies offer them, but consumers often fail to install them. This poses an interesting challenge for innovators: how can you motivate people to install updates? Apple's approach is to keep the process as easy as possible. They notify you that an update will be installed in the middle of the night while you're asleep. All you have to do is give your permission. In doing so, Apple removed all friction from the update process. Tesla takes another approach. They seduce car owners to install updates by packing them with new, desirable features. People download software updates to get the new features, while their car's security gets updated simultaneously.

Make it Traceable

No matter how good their security is, products can always get stolen. Luckily, connected products are increasingly easy to track. Apple was one of the first to implement this in mobile devices with their 2010 launch of the "Find my iPhone" feature. Now, many connected products implement these features, enabling the development of new value-added services. With the integration of location tracking tech into their bikes, electric bike manufacturer VanMoof offers an optional anti-theft guarantee. If your bike goes missing, you can report it as stolen in the bike's app. VanMoof's Bike Hunters have two weeks to recover your bike. If they can't, VanMoof will replace your bike with one of equal or better age and condition.

DOS & DON'TS

O If you want to make security core to your product's positioning, also have a look at Preserve Data Privacy (R2) and Offer Transparency (R3). They can reinforce your security features.

O Know your consumers. How high is security on their list of priorities? Design accordingly.

O Don't assume that security is one-size-fits-all. As there is often a trade-off between security and ease of use, it is wise to give people options to choose from without making things overly complicated.

R5 INCREASE CONTROL

Today, our lives are filled with products and services meant to make our lives easier and more convenient. They enable us to do things we couldn't do before. The sheer number of options, settings, and intangible elements that digital products offer can infringe on people's sense of control over their products and lives. Using an app to lock your car can leave you wondering if it's really locked. How can you ensure your kids don't see something unsuited for their age while surfing the web? Returning a sense of control through design can be achieved through the following tactics:

Add Overview

Keeping track of the sheer number of smart devices in our lives can be overwhelming. From playing music to brewing coffee, there is an app or voice command for everything. Without a clear overview, people can feel they lack control. The app Homey makes it easier to control all of your connected devices from one app by providing an overview. Left the lights on? Afraid the oven's still running? Check with Homey. Their "Flows" feature offers you control through sequences of pre-programmed instructions for your devices. Like a wake-up alarm triggering the coffee machine and opening the blinds, Flows can be programmed however you like.

Add Suggestions

While new technologies introduce new benefits, they can also introduce new anxieties. Take electric cars, whose introduction necessitated a global system of charging stations. The term "range anxiety" only caught on as electric cars did. Tesla addresses this anxiety by allowing you to map your routes past their charging stations, ensuring that you'll never get stranded. Although drivers can still decide otherwise, Tesla took the weight of route planning off of the drivers, which is especially helpful when you're in unknown territory.

Add Sensory Feedback

When using digital products, many people are uncertain whether they're on or off. This holds particularly true for products that make use of cameras or microphones. How can you be sure the webcam is off? Anybody who has made a video conference call has experienced that sinking feeling of forgetting whether or not their mic is muted. Many people can't help but repeatedly check that they're muted throughout a call. In these situations, sensory feedback provides peace of mind. Apple's Macbooks display a bright green light whenever the FaceTime camera is active.

Discord is an online voice, video, and chat communication platform. When voice or video chat is enabled in Discord on Mac, a small circle appears on the menu bar. The circle lights up to indicate to people when their microphone is detecting sound. Sometimes, it's the little things that make a big difference.

Add Manual Control

While many virtual products and services offer great benefits, the software behind them can make them seem mysterious. For example, smart home technology's convenience is often trumped by people's fear of the unknown software behind them. A Parks Associates survey shows that 79% of US households fear that smart home devices lead to data security and privacy issues. Candle, a privacy-friendly smart home concept, gave their devices big red switches, allowing people to manually turn them on and off. This physical act gives Candle's users a sense of control over their smart home devices. Webcam covers have become widely used due to the same principle. Slide the cover out of camera view for meetings, and slide it back when you're done. Webcam covers are a cheap, easy way for people to achieve physical control over their webcam.

Add Levels of Control

Enabling families to set different levels of control for each member can can bring peace of mind to users, particularly parents. For example, families with smart security systems can assign rights to different types of users. While parents can view video feeds and remotely open doors, kids can only turn the system on or off. Cleaners may be limited to disabling the system at specified times throughout the week. Another example is products that enable families to control who can do what online. Various internet providers offer pre-set content filters based on age, enabling parents to control what their kids are exposed to.

Give Detailed Control

Some online experiences have seemed beyond our control for ages. Google advertisements have become as familiar to us as breathing. We have grown used to personalized ads selling us whatever we searched for shortly before. Few consumers are aware that Google gives you control over the "interests" they use to personalize your ads and that they also explain how they arrived at each of them. You can disable every interest individually, giving you (some) control over the type of ads displayed, or turn them off all at once.

Special

" Writing this book completely messed up my Google profile. I see ads for products I would never buy."

Deborah Nas

45-54 years old	Female	Music Streams & Downloads	Network Security
Idomoo	Advertising & Marketing	News	Nintendo
Amsterdam	Android OS	Online Image Galleries	Online Video
Anime & Manga	Apparel	Outdoors	Parental Status: 3 factors
Apple iOS	Architecture	Parenting	Pest Control
Athletic Apparel	Athletic Shoes	Pets	Photographic & Digital Arts
Audio Equipment	Auto Brakes	Power Supplies	Price Comparisons
Auto Insurance	Autos & Vehicles	Primary & Secondary Schooling ...	Printers, Copiers & Fax Machines
Bars, Clubs & Nightlife	Beauty & Fitness	Product Reviews & Price Compa...	Recruitment & Staffing
Bedding & Bed Linens	Bicycles & Accessories	Restaurants	Retail Equipment & Technology
Blues	Boating	Retirement & Pension	Rugby
Science Fiction & Fantasy Films	Search Engines	Running & Walking	School Supplies & Classroom Eq...
Security Products & Services	Shopping	Insurance	Investing
Shopping Portals	Signage	Jazz	Job Industry: 4 factors
Skins, Themes & Wallpapers	Smart Phones	Job Listings	Jobs
Soccer	Social Networks	Lamps & Lighting	Language Resources
Soft Drinks	Software	Laptops & Notebooks	Luxury Goods
Soul & R&B	Speakers	Mac OS	Maps
Sports	Stock Photography	Marital Status: Married	Mass Merchants & Department ...
Stocks & Bonds	Swimming	Mobile & Wireless	Mobile Apps & Add-Ons
Tablet PCs	Teaching & Classroom Resources	Mobile Phones	Monitoring Software
Technical Support & Repair	Tesla Motors	Motor Vehicles (By Brand)	Motor Vehicles (By Type)
Translation Tools & Resources	Travel & Transportation	Movie & TV Streaming	Movies
Books & Literature	Bread Makers		
Broadcast & Network News	Building Materials & Supplies		

Financial Market
Fitness Technolo
Footwear
Foreign Languag
Gourmet & Speci
Graphics & Anim
Greeting Cards
Hockey
Home & Interior
Home Automatic
Home Improveme
Hybrid & Alterna
Computer Memo
Computer Scienc
Consumer Electr
Coupons & Disco
Currencies & For
Cycling
Desktop Comput
Digital Currencie
Education
Electrical Test &
Family Films

R6 ENSURE COMPATIBILITY

Incompatibility between products has long been a significant source of concern for consumers. Incompatibility has both physical and digital causes, like different connectors or different data formats. Prospective buyers of new tech products may wonder if that tech will work with the products they own or plan on buying. Can they play old games on their new console? Will that phone support the smartwatch they intend to buy? Limited compatibility can also restrict consumers' freedom of choice for future purchases. Hesitant buyers may ask if they're stuck with that brand forever. They may wonder about the geographic compatibility of the product. Can I use 5G abroad? Am I allowed to stream this content when I travel?

When there are too many questions around a product's compatibility, consumers will be hesitant to adopt it. You can use the following tactics to improve your product's compatibility:

Facilitate Backwards Compatibility

When purchasing new tech products, one of the hardest things to justify for consumers is the immediate inability to use their previously compatible accessories and peripherals. Apple is infamous for its poor backwards compatibility. In 2016, they removed the headphone jack from their new smartphones. Every wired set of headphones on the market was no longer iPhone compatible without using Apple's headphone jack adapter. When they updated their Macbook Pro

Prospective buyers of new tech products may wonder if that tech will work with the products they own or plan on buying

lineup in 2016, Apple removed all USB-A ports from the computer. Users who upgraded to the new Macbook also had to purchase expensive adapters and docking stations to continue using their peripherals. Sony's Playstations, on the other hand, are an example of excellent backwards compatibility. If you buy the new PS5, nearly all of your PS4 games will still be playable. Sonos offers a separate device, the Sonos Amp, that connects to your old analog speakers and fully integrates them into your Sonos wireless home sound system.

Facilitate Guest Use

If geographic limitations prohibit you from providing your service everywhere, roaming might be an option. Roaming means the facilitation of guest use and originates in the mobile phone business. Mobile phone operators have standardized infrastructure and bilateral contracts that allow people to use their mobile phones in different countries with a single mobile phone plan. When people cross a border, they are logged in that country as a guest user and are automatically connected to the service. Any calling costs you make are settled via your own provider; you never have to pay more than one bill.

Operators of charging stations for electric cars allow customers of other operators to roam their charging networks. Tesla cars are compatible with these public charging networks, allowing drivers to charge anywhere they like. In addition, Tesla developed their own standard for super-fast charging. This proprietary standard is not licensed to other car manufacturers, and adapters are not available. As a result, other cars can't charge at Tesla's supercharger stations. By investing heavily in quickly expanding its supercharger networks, offering speed as a powerful benefit over regular charging stations, and offering free charging to Tesla owners for years, Tesla used noncompatibility as a competitive advantage.

Facilitate API Connectivity

Each time you use an app to check the weather, reserve a table at a restaurant, or control your smart home devices, you're using an API: an Application Programming Interface. An API is a software interface that allows two applications to talk to each other. It defines which calls or requests can be made, how to make them, which data formats must be used, and many other things. These days, creating an API is the most popular way to enable third-party compatibility and interoperability with your product or platform.

IFTTT, short for If This Then That, is a software platform that opens up a world of possibilities to connect your product to other products. IFTTT uses APIs to link numerous connected products together in trigger-based automated flows, promising consumers to "help all their products and services work better together." For example, these flows can automatically add all tracks from Spotify's Discover Weekly to a designated playlist or automatically turn lights on at sunset. Possibilities are endless, and there is no coding involved. IFTTT enables users to connect previously incompatible products and platforms.

An API is also a useful tool for enabling third party compatibility with your products. Many companies striving to build an ecosystem of smart products launch a partner program. Nest, Google's smart thermostat, initially launched a successful partner program called "Works with Nest" to enable other smart home systems to "take what Nest knows and personalize your experience, such as turning

Seamless Setup Badge

off the lights when you're away." After Google acquired Nest, Works with Nest was parked. Nest is now part of "Works with Hey Google" (WWHG), a program intended to help Google Assistant control all your connected products. Google offers branding guidelines and various badges to companies that join the partner program. The "Seamless Setup badge," for example, indicates that a product can be set up using the Google Home app. No third-party apps are needed at all.

An API is a software interface that allows two applications to talk to each other. It is a useful tool for enabling third party compatibility with your products

Facilitate Data Exchange

A 2016 publication of Scientific Data saw the introduction of the "FAIR Guiding Principles for scientific data management and stewardship." These principles were meant to improve the Findability, Accessibility, Interoperability, and Reuse of digital assets. While FAIR is not a standard, its principles are used in that context. In the medical field, healthcare data is compiled and stored at a massive scale. The use of this

data has yet to reach its full potential, as it is stored in different ways and in different places. The Personal Health Train seeks to increase the usefulness of existing data by connecting it into one comprehensive data set. Standardizing data storage according to FAIR guidelines makes it findable, accessible, interoperable, and retrievable by individuals, hospitals, physicians, and public or private data repositories across the healthcare industry. Storing your data according to FAIR principles can make it compatible across multiple platforms, potentially adding value for your customers.

Facilitate the Creation of New Standards

Standards battle with each other in the early development stages of new markets. As a result, people may wonder if a product's underlying technology is or will become compatible with the future market standard and be hesitant to buy such a product. A decade ago, manufacturers pushing 3 TVs encountered this exact problem. Different standards for the glasses that created the 3D effect made consumers unsure of what to buy and hampered the availability of 3D content.

For upcoming technologies, forming a consortium of industry leaders and governmental bodies is common practice to develop new standards. As 5G is quickly becoming the standard for cellular networks, leading telecom companies and hardware/software manufacturers have involved themselves in the creation of standards and regulations. Another example is hyperloop, an ultra-high-speed transportation network. Hardt Hyperloop, Europe's leading hyperloop development company, is partnering with other hyperloop companies to set a European standard. The European Committee for Standardization (CEN) leads this joint effort.

Facilitate Compatibility Across Platforms

Many manufacturers choose to create a "lockin" with consumers by limiting the expansion of a system of connected tech products to their own brand(s). However, this is not in the best interest of consumers and might hold people back from buying the system in the first place. Systems and products that are compatible with other brands offer people freedom of choice. For example, Apple Watch owners looking to switch from an iPhone to a Samsung Galaxy will lose the option to sync their watch's activity and health data. The Apple Watch is incompatible with Android. On the other hand, a Fitbit is compatible with both iOS and Android, offering its owners much more freedom of choice.

DOS & DON'TS

O Joining existing platforms and partner programs is an excellent way to connect to product ecosystems and grow compatibility.

O If possible, work with APIs. It's the easiest way to achieve compatibility.

O Identify other parties offering the same service you do in domains you can't access. Consider a partnership that could bridge the gap between those domains.

O Don't ignore your customer's past investments. Strive to make your products backwards compatible with peripherals and accessories. Your customers will thank you for it.

R7 BE FUTURE-PROOF

In the world of tech, products come and go. Unfortunately, many go sooner than necessary. A well-known, albeit infamous term these days, is "planned obsolescence." To ensure future profits, some companies design their products with a limited useful life to become obsolete within a predetermined period of time.

Aware that their products will eventually become outdated, many people seek solutions to keep their products viable for longer. The following tactics can help make your product more future-proof:

Offer Accessories

Accessories can allow for future expansion of a product's functionality. To lower their initial costs, people can first buy a basic product, then decide to add accessories later. Today, for example, many people see limited value in controlling their coffee machines with their smartphones. As a result, they are unwilling to pay extra for a coffee machine with that feature included. However, as their friends start using the growing number of coffee machines equipped with smartphone control, people may experience the benefits of app-initiated, easy-to-program personalized coffee recipes. Jura, a maker of specialty coffee machines, offers its customers the option to buy a Smart Connect accessory that can be plugged into your machine for instant smartphone control.

Offer Future-Ready Hardware

Future features you are planning to launch might require special hardware. By preemptively implementing this hardware in your products now, a simple software update will be enough to unlock the latest functionality for your customer.

> Aware that their products will eventually become outdated, many people seek solutions to keep their products viable for longer

However, such implementation may backfire without clear communication to customers. Owners of the Google Nest Guard were shocked when Google announced that the product would receive voice-activated Google Assistant functionality. Before the announcement, they had no idea that the Nest Guard had a microphone.

Shortly after Tesla's mid-2017 Tesla Model 3 launch, people noticed a driver-facing camera above the rearview mirror. In spring 2019, one customer tweeted Elon Musk, demanding an answer. In response, Musk tweeted[45]: "It's there for when we start competing with Uber/Lyft & people allow their car to earn money for them as part of the Tesla shared autonomy fleet. In case someone messes up your car, you can check the video." While this is not yet a reality, Tesla announced in a 2020 tweet that its next software release would enable car owners to use the camera for something else. By turning on the camera, car owners can help Tesla engineers develop safety features and enhancements in the future[46]. If enabled, this feature would share a short video clip from the moments before and after an accident. Tesla promised that video clips "will not be associated with your Vehicle Identification Number to protect your privacy."

Neither Google nor Tesla explained the inactive hardware that would enable future features, but the user response differed significantly. This is due to a few reasons. First, many people distrust Google, while Tesla owners are almost "religious followers." Second, while the microphone was not visible to users, the camera was. As a result, people started asking questions soon after the product launch, when only a few people had managed to get their hands on the coveted Model 3. Finally, Tesla is easy to approach; Musk himself replies to tweets about the companies' innovations.

Offer Upgrades

People looking to buy a product that will last well into the future often consider how easily the product's hardware and software can be upgraded. The Mac Pro, Apple's pricey workstation, makes performance their value proposition. There is no preconfigured model; the product is fully customizable, and most importantly, can be modified and upgraded later on. The product is designed to allow you to open the casing with one hand, in one single movement, revealing the workstation's modules, which are deliberately placed in an easy-to-reach manner. When higher performance modules become available and users need more computing power, they can upgrade or add modules.

When your product consists of multiple individual devices working together in one system, consider consolidating your intelligence or computing power into a central device. This allows you to make your "edge devices" affordable, and future-proof. For example, when designing a smart home system, you can upgrade the hub to upgrade the entire systems' functionality. Allow customers to connect their existing smart edge devices to the new hub and benefit from the new functionality. People with Philips Hue bulbs installed throughout their homes can unlock various additional features just by upgrading the

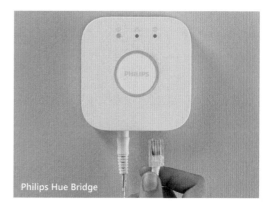

Philips Hue Bridge

brain of their smart lighting system's central hub. Transitioning from Hue Bridge v1 to Hue Bridge v2 unlocks new, free features not supported by Hue Bridge v1, like compatibility with Apple's HomeKit, Hue Entertainment and voice support for Amazon Alexa and Google Assistant.

Offer Ongoing Functionality

Connected products can make us dependent on the cloud services that enable their functionality. As a result, we depend on the companies offering those services. When it comes to startups, people might lack confidence in a company's continued support. The startup could go bankrupt or be acquired at any time. Two years after acquiring the smart home startup Revolv, Google Nest announced that it would be permanently shutting down its smart home hub. Users of Revolv's hub were left with a non-functioning, useless device. By ensuring that your products can function in a stand-alone setting, not reliant on any cloud services, you can reassure people of their products' usefulness regardless of your company's existence. Since functionality in a stand-alone setting is most likely limited, you must be transparent about this.

As it ages, eventually a product's hardware will not be able to deliver the performance that new software relies on. Apple has been accused of planned obsolescence as they deliberately slowed the performance of older model iPhones following a software upgrade to a new operating system. Apple, though, argued that they did this to "prolong the life" of phones. They included battery management capabilities to prevent old phones from unexpected shutdowns resulting

from the increased processing power that the new operating system required. Nevertheless, Apple agreed to pay well over $100 million in settlements in what became known as "batterygate." Regulators argued that consumers "were not informed that installing iOS updates could slow down their devices" and Apple had not provided customers with an "effective way to recover the full functionality of their devices."

Over time, Apple has improved the compatibility of old models with new iOS releases. While the first two iPhone releases could only support two major iOS updates, later models could support five to six. The iPhone 6S was launched with iOS 9 in 2015 and will still be compatible with this year's iOS 14[47]. While Apple does not currently use this as a marketing tactic, advertising this kind of device longevity could allay people's concerns about expensive products quickly becoming outdated.

When offering upgrades through the release of new operating systems, carefully consider which products can and cannot support these. There's a fine line between offering your customers access to the latest features and making their devices too slow to comfortably use. One solution can be to let your customers reinstall their previous operating system if they dislike the new one, another can be to simply not make the new operating system available to customers with models too old to support it. In the latter case, you should continue to serve them with security updates for their "old" operating system.

Offer Your Product as a Service

When consumers buy a product, they weigh their investment against the duration of use. If they expect a product to quickly become outdated or broken, they might shy away from the purchase. More and more, consumers prefer not to buy a product but to get a service instead. While more expensive over time, services do offer benefits. Besides the promise of a product that always works, it also lowers the risks that come with outdated technology. If you pay a monthly fee to use an electric bike or a smart washing machine, you can easily upgrade when newer models offer more desirable features. For more information on Product-as-a-Service models, read the special on Product-Service systems on page 50.

read the special on Product-Service systems on page 50.

DOS & DON'TS

○ Think carefully about your product roadmap and equip today's products with the right components to support future services.

○ Explore possibilities for a modular product design. It's an excellent way to accommodate upgrades and accessories.

○ Seriously consider offering your product as a service. It will make future-proofing products in your own best interest.

○ Don't accept planned obsolescence. If your company considers it, speak up and convince people otherwise.

There's a fine line between offering your customers access to the latest features and making their devices too slow to comfortably use

R8 COMPLY WITH REGULATIONS

Doing business is not possible without regulatory compliance. Achieving this, however, is harder than it sounds. Regulations change all the time. The unintended side effects of products and technologies can force regulators to respond with new laws and regulations. For example, problems caused by badly parked shared bikes led to bike-parking regulations. Big tech's data-based business models led to the new European Digital Services Act. Innovators need to be prepared to adjust their products in order to ensure compliance as regulations change. The following tactics can help you identify and comply with current and future regulations:

Meet Local Regulations

Differences in local regulations can force you to adapt your product, business model, or even your infrastructure. For example, as data sovereignty dictates that all data converted and stored within a country is subject to that country's data use laws, you might need to adapt your privacy policies locally and set up your infrastructure to accommodate this. While WhatsApp shares US user data with Facebook, the data of European citizens is protected.

Though incredibly popular in cities across the globe, electric scooters are not available everywhere. In the Netherlands, electric scooters are not allowed on the road. They are classified in the same category as other motor scooters, and as such, must comply with 46 different regulatory articles. Micro, an e-scooter company, figured out how to re-classify the scooters. As long as a handlebar throttle can't power them, the scooters are no longer considered "motor scooters." For the scooters they sell in the Netherlands, Micro digitally disables the throttle and uses the motor to provide "step-powered" assistance, thereby catering to local regulations.

Meet Future Regulations

Since regulations are usually preceded by long public debates, you can often anticipate what's coming. For example, as speed pedelecs become faster and more popular, their impact on dense urban transportation is growing. This will likely call for increased speed regulations on e-bikes, enforced by geofences that detect and limit the bikes' speeds within certain zones. In anticipation of this, pedelec producers could design them with built-in GPS speed regulators, automatically capping the bike's speed where necessary.

In preparation for new-to-the-world product launches, companies most often need to lobby for regulation change. Failure to do so might lead to major setbacks. Segway's original personal electric transporter didn't fit into any existing vehicle class. As a result, law enforcers didn't know how to deal with them; some riders got fined, and others were tolerated. Combined, the Segway's high price and uncertain regulatory situation convinced many consumers that the purchase was too risky. The Segway never went mainstream.

Enforce Regulation Compliance

While your product may be compliant with regulations, your company may still be held accountable for users who misbehave or break the rules. Bike-sharing companies encountered massive opposition from citizens and municipalities when riders began dumping their bikes everywhere. A growing number of cities are forcing bike sharing companies to implement customer behavior steering measures. Apps show riders where they can and cannot park; repeat parking violators will be fined or blocked from future use. Some cities require bike companies to use geofencing in order to forbid users to end their bike rental if they park the bike in a no-parking zone. As users pay per minute, there is a strong incentive to park the bike in the right place.

New regulations in China limit the time and money that kids under 16 can spend on video games. Gameplay is forbidden between 10:00 PM and 8:00 AM. Depending on their age, kids can spend a maximum of 200 to 400 yuan on games per month. Game companies are responsible for enforcing these rules. Determining how to enforce regulations like these can be challenging and should be considered during the design process.

DOS & DON'TS

O Actively inform yourself about regulations on every level. Overlooking regulations can lead to many problems.

O For new-to-the-world products, there is a fair chance you will run into regulatory challenges. Involve policymakers and other regulatory stakeholders early on in the innovation process.

O Design with both current and future regulations in mind.

O Don't assume your users will comply. Build regulation compliance mechanisms into your product or service.

R9 BUILD PARTNERSHIPS

New tech products tend to come with many uncertainties for users. The technology could fail to deliver promised results, quality may be poor, and the overall product's effectiveness might be low. Manufacturers often overpromise and underdeliver. As a result, many people are hesitant to adopt new tech products. Hesitance to adopt your products can be mitigated by partnering with established organizations or trustworthy brands. Partnerships can speed up the development of standards and markets and build trust with consumers.

The younger the company and technology behind the product, the more people question whether buying that product is such a good idea. With startups, people become even more cautious. Naturally, startups are not the only parties who benefit from partnering with other companies or brands. The following tactics can help any company of any age take advantage of partnerships:

Partner With Government

Partnering with a governmental organization can give your product instant legitimacy. For startups, joining a "startups in residence" program is the easiest way to do so. Many large cities have such startup accelerator programs, designed to allow collaborations between cities and startups. ECO coin offers people digital coins for sustainable behaviors like installing solar panels or riding a bike to work. These coins can be spent on sustainable experiences and circular products. By joining Amsterdam's startups in residence programs, ECO coin created consumer awareness through free publicity. Simultaneously, people's hesitance to use digital wallets will be mitigated by the government's endorsements.

The public assumption is that government-company partnerships have society's best interests in mind. When this assumption doesn't match up with the partnership's reality, resistance against your product will increase. Ring is a smart doorbell company owned by Amazon. It comes with the Neighbors app, which allows people to share information and recordings of suspicious activity within the community. In 2019, Ring announced a partnership with law enforcement, promising to help solve neighborhood crime. However, while seemingly innocent, this partnership has a dark side. Police can request access to footage from homeowners, effectively turning Ring into an expansive public surveillance network. Though Ring doesn't disclose the nature of its partnership with law enforcement, it has sustained many public attacks for these policies.

Partner With Nonprofits

When commercial organizations set out to tackle larger societal issues besides their normal business operations, consumers may have difficulty believing their actions are ethically motivated. Partnering with nonprofits can legitimize a company's good intentions. Multiple drone startups are partnering with Unicef to address humanitarian supply chain systems and delivery and improve connectivity in hard-to-reach communities. The open-source drone technology these startups are developing for Unicef adds credibility to their intentions. Furthermore, it positively affects their companies' reputations and improves the overall image of the drone product category.

Partner With Strong Brands

Consumers' trust in a product's efficacy, security, or trustworthiness can be enhanced by partnerships with strong brands. In 2019, Apple partnered with Mastercard to offer their own credit card. Issued by Goldman Sachs, the Apple Card is primarily used with Apple Pay functionality. Apple's partnership with Mastercard preemptively addressed fears that the Apple Card would not be secure. Apple Card uses "Mastercard's technology in conjunction with Apple and Goldman Sachs" to facilitate a "new kind of consumer experience," according[48] to Mastercard's founder.

Partner With Suppliers

As technology progresses, the number of constituent parts that make up a product grows as well. Part suppliers can partner with reputable companies to convey to people the quality of their products. Intel's "Intel Inside" program put their processors on the map by partnering with the computer companies using their processors. They became the first computer chip manufacturer to advertise directly to consumers. As a result, the Intel name became a badge of performance, boldly displayed by the computers using their chips.

Partner With Competitors

Companies can compete head-to-head in the marketplace while simultaneously working together to set new standards or tackle a societal problem. Though Apple and FitBit are fierce competitors in the wearables market, they are now collaborating in a consortium that sets out to learn how data from wearables can identify and track infectious diseases like Covid-19.

BMW, Ford, and other technology companies are joining forces in an initiative led by the Mobility Open Blockchain Initiative to develop blockchain-based "birth certificates" for cars. In the future, this will allow consumers and everyone in the value chain to track a car's maintenance history, mileage records, damages, and everything else, all the way from manufacturing to end owner.

HARDT HYPERLOOP

The hyperloop is a new and sustainable high-speed transportation mode for passengers and cargo. In 2013, Elon Musk published a 58-page document detailing his idea: a low-pressure tube system for vehicles traveling at high speeds. He then invited multidisciplinary student teams to join a prototyping contest. Delft University of Technology's team won the contest and founded Hardt Hyperloop, one of Europe's leading hyperloop development companies. Hyperloop presents a rare opportunity to study the acceptance and resistance of a new-to-the-world mobility concept as it unfolds.

Hyperloop offers many benefits. It enables emission-free travel at airplane speeds, using only 10% of the energy. The system is low maintenance due to tubes that protect the system from weather, as well as friction-free magnetic levitation, propulsion, and lane-switching technologies. Compared with trains, hyperloop's small infrastructure footprint can be easily integrated into existing landscapes and transport hubs. High speeds and lack of intermediate stops reduce travel time, regularly departing vehicles increase flexibility, and the magnetic levitation enables smooth rides.

Studies[49] show that hyperloop is economically and financially viable for a European network. Combined with the benefits mentioned above, it is a promising alternative to high-speed rail and short-haul flights.

The hyperloop is made up of proven technologies that, when combined, create an entirely new mode of transport. Nevertheless, as with any new-to-the-world product, hyperloop has been met with resistance from the beginning. Three clusters of arguments drive this resistance. The first questions the technology's safety and feasibility. Self-proclaimed experts deem hyperloop unsafe, impossible, or too expensive. Some ask, assuming that synthetic kerosine will fuel airplanes in the future, "what problem are we solving?" The second cluster addresses the physical discomfort that travelers might experience due to acceleration, deceleration, and a lack of windows. The third focuses on environmental and societal effects; the hyperloop requires new infrastructure, and people who can travel faster will travel more.

While each of these resistances can be countered by technical and economic arguments, adoption won't happen overnight. Hardt Hyperloop does not take this reality lightly.

Accounting for possible resistance from the very beginning, they adopted an ecosystem approach. They initiated the Hyperloop Development Program, through which hyperloop companies, industry, government, and research institutes work towards European standardization of hyperloop technologies and regulation. Together with experts and partners, Hardt is also constructing a European Hyperloop Center to develop and test hyperloop technologies. Furthermore, they are forming a consortium of market partners to create the first hyperloop cargo route. Finally, Hardt Hyperloop uses consumer research to develop a better product. So far, they have achieved great results. The Dutch government and the European Commission are fully on board, and product development is speeding ahead.

Hardt Hyperloop

R10 FIT SOCIAL NORMS

Companies whose products oppose and disrupt social norms often raise public resistance and, at some point, may even be forced to retract their product from the market. You must anticipate the possibility that your product will not fit into social norms and identify the resulting pushback. The following tactics can help you identify the effect social norms may have on your product and improve your product's design to minimize possible resistance:

Address Cultural Differences

Culture describes the ideas, customs, and social behavior of a particular group of people or society. Culture can vary significantly and is not governed by national borders. It is also a layered concept; within each culture, there are subcultures, and so on. When developing new tech products, considering their cultural context is critical for success. Our social norms and behavior around dating, for example, are very culture-sensitive. The dating app Tinder was hugely successful in the US and Europe, where casual dating is normal. In Asia, on the other hand, the app found little interest. In many countries, sex before marriage is unacceptable. This is why Tinder chose to take a different approach for Asia, positioning itself as a social app for generation Z. At the beginning of 2021, the company launched a campaign in Thailand called "Friends with (Other) Benefits." Here, they explain – with a bit of humor – that Tinder is not a dating app; it's an app to find people with shared interests; new friends with whom you can share fun activities like gaming or visiting a museum. Such a different positioning is, of course, not just marketing; Tinder's product itself is also different in these countries, both interface and algorithm.

Address Product Perception

Many products and categories are misjudged or misunderstood. For example, parents tend to worry if their kids engage in gaming, as many see gaming as an addictive, socially isolated activity. The reality is very different, though; many games are highly social. But because many games look like traditional shooter games, like Fortnite does, outsiders don't perceive them as social. Minecraft, one of the world's most popular games, was very successful at keeping product perception in mind while designing their game. Minecraft stimulates creativity, teaches kids how to work together in teams, and helps them practice their problem-solving and project management skills. They even learn the fundamentals of programming. Minecraft chose a look and feel that sets it apart from other games, contributing to its social acceptance.

Address Misapplication

Anticipating the social problems your product could cause will help you create solutions for them early on. Electric scooters are a good example of complying with regulations while disregarding social norms. Widespread use of rentable smart scooters has left them littered all over city streets. Spin, a scooter startup recently acquired by Ford, aims to solve this problem with their 3-wheeled smart scooter. Spin's self-repositioning software, combined with front and rear-facing cameras, enables the scooters to be remotely controlled and relocated in an orderly fashion. They hope that their compliance with social norms will give them a notable advantage over other smart scooter fleets.

Support Societal Challenges

A product's ability to address larger societal challenges can make us reevaluate our disapproval of it on a product level. For example, in western cultures, we tend to disapprove of robots replacing humans for social interaction. Many people frown upon social robots for elderly people, even if the elderly themselves are happy with them. However, when framed in the context of higher-level benefits, these products become more acceptable.

Social robots like ElliQ help fight loneliness, a growing problem among the elderly. The social robot also reminds people to drink water, take their medicine, plays memory-training games, or stimulates people to do some simple exercises. This means less pressure on retirement home staff, allowing them to spend their time providing better care. When people understand the win-win, social acceptance can grow.

Support Societal Concerns

Even when not required to do so by regulatory bodies, many companies make decisions that align with public or societal concerns. IBM, Amazon, and Microsoft have all announced they'll stop selling their facial recognition technology to law enforcement until federal laws regulating its use are instated. Apple has also shown they care about the public's privacy concerns. During a 2014 investigation, the FBI asked Apple for help unlocking a suspect's iPhone. By refusing, Apple was cemented in many people's eyes as a security-forward company.

ElliQ

R11 MAKE IT (IN)VISIBLE

Product visibility is an essential aid in increasing product recognition and adoption speed. Visibility is relevant in a social context, where it facilitates creating awareness of a product's existence. It is also relevant in an individual context, where visible results from using the product reassure people about a product's efficacy. The following tactics will help you use (in)visibility as a driver for product adoption:

Attract Attention

Some products make such an impression that they market themselves. Either their look or their function stands out, making them intriguing and instantly recognizable. Segway took full advantage of product recognition potential with their Loomo Robot. It combines a hoverboard's functionality with cameras, AI, and autonomous movement capability to create a robot assistant that follows you around and obeys your every command. Its novel look and futuristic capabilities make the Loomo a conversation piece. When people see its functionality and how easy it is to ride, their curiosity makes them want to try it out. In this way, Loomo leveraged visibility to make their product a success.

Create a Signature Look & Feel

A product's look and feel can generate an irrefutable emotional or cognitive response. In some cases, recognizing a product takes just a glance. This is just as true for a sports car as it is for digital tools. Prezi, a virtual presentation software, was famous for its signature look and feel. Anybody could tell when a presentation was made in Prezi. Prezi's recognizability meant that it effectively marketed itself to consumers. After a surge of users, though, Prezi's popularity began to wane. Inspired by the current work-from-home demand, Prezi recently released a new video presentation tool, as instantly recognizable as its predecessor.

Make the Invisible Visible

Many products carry out invisible functions. Without sensory cues, users can be uncertain the product is actually doing its job. Smoke alarms periodically flash a light to visually assure users it has battery life and is working. Dyson, an appliance company, calms uncertainty about their air purifier's effectiveness using sensors and the Dyson app. A diagram in the app indicates the air's purity over time, displaying the purifier's effect on the room's air. This reassures users that the air in their room is indeed being purified.

Make the Visible Invisible

While some products benefit from standing out, others benefit from being invisible. Functional products, such as wearable medical devices, often send a message about the wearer. As a result, these vital products can be embarrassing to be seen with. Health and wellness companies are replacing embarrassing fall-monitoring pendants with modern smartwatches, helping the elderly protect themselves in a discreet manner. Sensors in the smartwatch guard against falls, track oxygen saturation and monitor heart rates. Another embarrassing safety device for the elderly is hip airbags, worn around the waist like a belt. The Wolk hip airbag alleviated embarrassment with their new airbag technology, allowing their protection device to be worn under clothing and out of sight. By making visible products invisible, these innovators removed the embarrassment hindering people from wearing potentially life-saving devices.

Make It Cool

Unless exposed products are designed to be invisible with understated colors and looks, they need to look great. Products that look cool can attract customers, or at the very least, looking cool can lower a product's adoption threshold. While light therapy glasses are not a new technology, their looks, coupled with uncertainty about their efficacy, has prevented them from catching on. Ayo took it upon themselves to develop cool-looking light therapy glasses, winning a Red Dot design award in the process. As options become more stylish, people are more willing to give the technology a try.

DOS & DON'TS

O If product visibility can help you to "help spread the message," design your product in such a way that it attracts attention for its looks or its functionality.

O Try to understand how people will feel when using your product. Be sensitive to consumers' insecurities; making functional products invisible can help to reduce user embarrassment.

O Be careful when choosing a signature style or color. For tech products, there is a fine line between desirability and putting people off.

O Don't just design for functionality; if your product is visible, it needs to look cool as well. Looks and functionality combined can add to your product's success.

R12 CREATE FAMILIARITY

Familiarity is a powerful design strategy essential for customer understanding of new tech's functionality. Design clues can help consumers link a new product to an existing category, enhancing their understanding of what the product is and how it works. The more novel your product and general your target audience, the more critical it is to consider familiarity as one of your design strategies. The following are three ways to design for product familiarity:

Balance Typicality and Novelty

Typicality describes the phenomenon whereby typical items are more easily judged as members of a category than atypical items. In other words, typicality increases recognizability. Novelty, on the other hand, evokes curiosity and enriches our experience. Research shows that consumers prefer products that optimally combine the opposing aesthetic forces of typicality and novelty[50]. In other words, we prefer products that are easily recognizable while offering something new. Designers call this design principle 'Most Advanced, Yet Acceptable' (MAYA, see following pages). The right balance between typicality and novelty varies per product category and per individual consumer. While this balance has yet to be researched for tech products, we can make some assumptions. Consumers often perceive purchasing highly innovative products as risky; there can be economic risks, performance risks, social risks, and more. Familiar designs can make consumers feel more comfortable buying these "risky" products[51]. Conversely, innovative tech in established product categories can be supplemented by novel, curiosity-triggering designs that attract consumers who are open to novelty.

The tech world is not short of novel products that created familiar designs. Many of Apple's designs resemble popular Braun electronics. Nest based their design on a hugely popular Honeywell thermostat (see page 152), and Tesla added a big plastic "grill" to their first release of the Model S even though this has no cooling functionality.

Leverage Mental Models

Repeated use of a product or interface causes users to build mental models encapsulating their understanding of how something works and is operated. When products look familiar to each other, people will expect them to operate in similar ways. We've all seen small children touching and swiping a TV screen, being surprised that "it's not working."

A mental model is based on beliefs, not facts, and can vary per individual and change over time. It is a key concept in human-computer interaction because it flattens the learning curve; it allows people to start using a product right away. This can lead to faster adoption rates, better usability, and improved overall experiences. To align with people's existing mental models, you should deep-dive into users' expectations of how your product will work.

For ease of use, stick to established mental models for websites, apps, etc. Keep in mind that they vary for users of different operating systems. Since the mental model concept is so common in UX design, similar features surface everywhere, given time. When Twitter introduced hashtags, Facebook and Instagram copied them. When Facebook introduced "Likes," LinkedIn and Instagram copied them. While users of competing apps benefit from this continued cycle due to decreased cognitive load, competitive differentiation decreases. Balancing the known and the new is vital.

Apply Skeuomorphism

Skeuomorphism is designing digital objects to mimic their real-world counterparts. Our computer's "trash can" is one of the most used skeuomorphic designs. The "save icon" in Microsoft word still looks like an old-fashioned floppy disc, even though its real-world counterpart is unrecognizable to young people.

Skeuomorphism is an effective tactic for new digital applications. Apple used this tactic at some point on most of their products. The first iPhone calculator app, for example, closely resembled the old, popular Braun ET44 calculator. When Apple launched their first version of the Books app, the interface looked like a picture of a wooden bookshelf. Several updates later, once people had embraced e-books, the interface transformed into a clean white design; the wooden bookshelves had vanished, with only rows of book thumbnails remaining.

DOS & DON'TS

O Decide if you want to link new-to-the-world products to an existing category or establish a new category. See page 24 for more details.

O Build on existing mental models to ensure ease of use, but also find ways to be unique.

O Using metaphors and analogies in your marketing strategy can create familiarity. See page 160 for more information.

O Implement design changes gradually with each new release.

O Don't make your product too novel. While it may satisfy your creative urge as an innovator, it may also lead to consumer confusion and uncertainty.

MAYA

Most Advanced
Yet Acceptable

Raymond Loewy (1983-1986) introduced the MAYA principle and used it to design the iconic Coca-Cola bottle, Air Force One, the Greyhound, and many other iconic designs. He literally revolutionized the industry, creating product designs for everything from packaging and refrigerators to cars and spacecraft. Referred to by the press as "The Man Who Shaped America," Loewy mastered striking the right balance between the present (what people know and are comfortable with) and the future (the innovative and unknown).

Loewy's MAYA principle tells us to design for the future but deliver this future gradually. If your product's design is too different, people will not feel comfortable using it and will likely reject it, even if your product is better than current solutions.

The early iPod is an excellent example of how Apple applied the MAYA principle. The first iPod in 2001 featured traditional buttons and included design elements that (subconsciously) linked it to CD players. Then, Apple's designers gradually pushed the product's design: the iPod gradually "lost" buttons and acquired a more streamlined interface. Although there is no way to prove it, many believe that without iPods paving the way, the iPhone would not have been as successful at launch."

" The adult public's taste is not necessarily ready to accept the logical solutions to their requirements if the solution implies too vast a departure from what they have been conditioned into accepting as the norm[52]."

Raymond Loewy

NEST LEARNING THERMOSTAT

The Nest Learning Thermostat is a great example of a product that integrates multiple design strategies. Specifically, two strategies play a key role in the thermostat's positioning: Save Money (B9) and Make It Simple (B3).

When Nest launched in 2011, most thermostats consisted of rubber buttons and colorless screens framed by cheap, white plastic covers. They were as hard to program as they were ugly. Despite their energy usage changing over time, most consumers installed their thermostat and never once altered the settings. The result was a waste of money and energy.

Nest changed all this. They created a thermostat that stood out for its simplicity, due to its clean, attractive design and a straightforward interface. It programs itself based on your living patterns to help save energy costs in the simplest way possible.

Another design strategy instrumental in Nest's success is Create Familiarity (R12). Nest chose a design that people knew. Their thermostat closely resembled a hugely popular Honeywell thermostat launched in 1953, the T86 Round. Nest redesigned the T86 into the sleek disk perched on your wall today that you need only turn to adjust the temperature. The iconic design subconsciously communicated to consumers that the Nest Learning Thermostat, although packed with new technology, was as simple to use as the popular thermostat from the '50s.

Honeywell, of course, was unhappy that Nest had hijacked their design to position themselves as the leader of the new smart thermostat product category. In a 2014 retaliation effort, Honeywell launched the similarly designed Lyric thermostat, but never managed to equal Nest's success. That same year, Google acquired Nest for $3.2 billion. This acquisition caused resistance among some consumers, as Google can now combine people's energy usage data with other data sources to paint an even more comprehensive picture of their users. Furthermore, Google could sell the energy usage data to utility companies or other interested parties.

Key to Nest's success is its core benefit, a combination of the design strategies Save Money (B9) and Make It Simple (B3), which has previously been incompatible in terms of customer expectations. Besides the design strategies essential to its positioning, Nest used six other strategies to add value to their product.

B9 SAVE MONEY

Nest discovers patterns in your habits and programs itself to fit your lifestyle. If you're not at home, it turns the heat down. Savings: up to 12% on heating bills and 15% on cooling bills.

B3 MAKE IT SIMPLE

Preprogrammed and button free, Nest learns what temperature you prefer and builds its schedule around your schedule.

R12 CREATE FAMILIARITY

The design builds on the iconic design of the T86 Round, a popular and user-friendly Honeywell thermostat launched in 1953.

Nest Smart Thermostat

B2 Personalize

The Nest thermostat learns what temperatures you prefer throughout the day. It automatically adapts as your life and the seasons change.

B1 Customize

Users can customize the screen to light up as you walk in the room, displaying whatever you choose: the temperature, weather, or time.

B6 Enable Anytime, Anywhere

The Nest app enables you to control settings or temperature from anywhere.

Supporting Design Strategies

B17 Fuel Motivation
B5 Make It Hassle-Free
B10 Increase Efficiency

R13 DESIGN FOR MARKETING STRATEGIES

New tech adoption efforts can be powerfully aided by the right marketing strategies. When working on your product's design and marketing strategies in parallel, you will find that they influence each other. Integrating both from the start of your innovation process can help you better mitigate resistance against your product and the technology it uses. This Design Strategy lays out several tactics explaining how marketing and product innovation can reinforce each other.

Become a Thought Leader

Thought leadership is a marketing strategy that is not so much focused on your product but more on your knowledge and vision, enabling you to establish yourself as an expert in the market. Thought leadership can be especially beneficial if you're active in upcoming product categories. The unfamiliarity of new products in upcoming categories can cause consumers to question how they work, if they're any good, and what value they bring. As a thought leader, you proactively answer any question that your target audience might have. Establishing thought leadership can be done in a variety of ways.

Starting a movement is about sharing a future vision and getting people on board with it. Your product is simply a step towards that vision. Tesla's 2006 master plan communicated their ambitious vision very successfully. It laid out their plan to: create an expensive, low volume sports car, use that money to build a less expensive, medium volume car, and use that money to create an affordable, high-volume car. People bought into the vision and became brand ambassadors, viewing their car purchases as more than just a means of transportation. Following the Roadster, the Model S, and the Model X, Tesla realized their vision with the release of the affordable and accessible Model 3.

"Owning" a challenge is about having in-depth knowledge of a problem and its underlying causes and developing solutions to address this problem. Lexilife is a young company that aims to change the lives of dyslexic people. People with dyslexia are often misdiagnosed and can struggle in school and in the workplace. Recent scientific research indicates that dyslexic people have two dominant eyes instead of one, making letters look blurred or mirrored and hindering their reading. This research became the basis for Lexilight, an LED-pulsating and modulating light that compensates for the underlying problem and enables dyslexics to read faster, longer, and without eye strain. Lexilife explicitly claims thought leadership on dyslexia. They back their product with scientific research, educate the general public about dyslexia, and partner with dyslexia support organizations.

Lexlight

Demonstrating technical superiority is about the expert application of technology. Instead of focusing on a particular market or product category, application of technology becomes a core part of your brand DNA, leverageable across product categories. For Dyson, this is airflow. Airflow was at the core of Dyson's revolutionary bagless vacuum cleaners. Next, they expanded into fans and purifiers, engineering their machines to multiply and project air further than any other device. They then used this knowledge to develop the Dyson haircare range. Dyson's Supersonic hairdryer has an iconic ring-shaped head that links it to the design of their fans and purifiers. Although a new player in the haircare market, Dyson's reputation and thought leadership on airflow made people more than willing to accept the steep $400 price tag.

Design for Specific Use Cases

Use cases describe specific situations in which products can be used and are most often linked to particular target groups. Targeting specific use cases can help a company make consumers feel

> Targeting specific use cases can help a company make consumers feel that the product is suited for them. It can make consumers confident to use and be seen with the product

that the product is suited for them. It can make consumers confident to use and be seen with the product. Although this might narrow your initial target market, you are more likely to realize high adoption rates as your product is geared for their use case. Choose your first use case carefully; the strategies that reduce resistance among the people fitting the use case might increase other people's resistance.

The Netherlands is the frontrunner in bicycle innovation, topping the chart at 1.3 bicycles per person. Even the prime minister rides his bike to work in the Netherlands. Unsurprisingly, it became one of the first countries to see the rise of electric bikes. Bicycle manufacturer Sparta launched electric bikes around 20 years ago, targeting older people and promising them that these bikes would make cycling easier. Although popular among this target group, the bike's positioning inhibited the spill-over effect to other target groups. Electric bikes were seen as a product for old people; you would not want to be seen riding one as a younger person. About ten years ago, this began to change. New brands began designing cool-looking, high-tech e-bikes targeting young business professionals, positioning e-bikes as the healthy alternative to taking the car. In 2019, over 70% of all bike sales revenue in The Netherlands came from electric bike sales due to brands optimizing their e-bike's design and marketing for commuters.

Demonstrate Quality and Efficacy

Both new tech products and products offered by new entrants raise quality and efficacy questions. As these products are new, they have yet to prove themselves. Consumers and most of the people around them have yet to personally experience these products. They may wonder if products perform properly, if their functions are reliable, or how durable they are. Your marketing strategy and product design can address these concerns in various ways.

Offering exceptional warranties can remove uncertainties regarding your product's quality. They address people's perceptions of financial risk

Both new tech products and products offered by new entrants raise quality and efficacy questions

in case of product break-down and instill trust in the product's quality. Due to the reputation of low reliability that Korean cars had among Western consumers, Kia, a South Korean automotive manufacturer, began promising a 7-year, 150,000 km limited warranty with new vehicle purchases. Compared with the 3-year, 100,000 km warranty most other car manufacturers offer, Kia offers new car buyers immense peace of mind. Today, Korean vehicles are known for their reliability and offer warranties as a badge of honor.

Creating durable designs and explaining them well can convince people that your product will last. When Samsung announced groundbreaking folding screen technology with their Galaxy Fold release, many people were hesitant to buy it. The high price aside, they had little confidence in the folding mechanism's durability. Samsung addressed these concerns, redesigning the hinge and explaining their new design in great detail on their website and on YouTube, addressing every concern. In response to worries about dirt getting into the hinge, they explain[53]: "To sweep away these worries, we tried out over a hundred different ideas. The 99th try gave us a starting point for a solution and on the 108th try we invented what we now call the sweeper." They also link this idea to the mechanisms of vacuums, a durable product that people are familiar with. The video contains lots of technical images, exploded views, and animations of the hinge's internals to encourage trust in the product's quality.

Large, active user communities function as an indicator of the quality and efficacy of products that rely on peer-to-peer activity or user-generated content. Navigation app Waze is

Waze

appealing to many users for its active community base's large size. Gamification techniques stimulate users to report accidents, traffic, police speed traps, and more. Waze uses this information to offer a more precise and up-to-date route. Seeing other "Wazers," depicted as funny icons on the navigation screen, offers users a constant confirmation of Waze's active community. They can even message a nearby Wazer to notify them or send them a "beep," just for the fun of it.

Work with Product Endorsers

Endorsements can assure people that your product lives up to its promises and that your company is trustworthy; they show public support or approval. Lately, the rise of influencer marketing on social media has put endorsement in a bad light. Influencers like Kim Kardashian and Kylie Jenner earn up to a million dollars for a single endorsed Instagram post. These endorsements are pure marketing and change nothing about the product itself. There are more valuable forms of endorsement to consider in which product design and endorsement marketing go hand in hand.

Peer endorsement can be a potent marketing tool if integrated into your product features. Users help others get to know and experience the product. Waze, the navigation app mentioned earlier, created a product feature called "share drive" to inform the person you're visiting about your estimated arrival time and route progress. It messages them a link that allows them to see your drive on a map. This creates awareness for the Waze app, gives people unfamiliar with it their first hands-on experience with the product, and clearly demonstrates its value: a real-time updated route plan and highly accurate estimated time of arrival.

Involving experts in your product's development can give it immediate credibility. These experts will help you develop better products, as they are very demanding and critical users. Redison, a developer of connected drum products, explains their team is "composed mainly of drummers, guitarists and singers." They also involve a community of ambassadors, professional drummers and drum teachers, in product development, product testing, and marketing. Another example is Coronamelder, a tracing app developed by the Dutch government. To ensure the most privacy-secure solution possible and earn citizens' trust, they involved well-known privacy critics in their design and development process.

Co-branding is one of the most visible types of endorsement. To reach the world of performance-focused athletes, Apple partnered with Nike to release the Apple Watch Nike+. It combined the Apple watch's sensors and functionality with the community, athletic reach, and motivating power of the Nike+ Run Club app. With Nike's help, Apple gave the watches distinct bands with a high-performance look and feel and a unique watch face with the Nike+ Run Club app's functionality integrated. With one tap, runners wearing the Apple Watch Nike+ could start their run. As Apple's COO put it, "Apple Watch Nike+ takes performance tracking to a whole new level and we can't wait to bring it to the world's largest community of runners."

Apple Watch Nike+

Independent third-party endorsements that convince consumers of your product's quality or your company's commitment towards a goal can be achieved by certification. For example, obtaining a certificate from Climate Neutral, a nonprofit organization working to decrease global carbon emissions, can give customers trust in your commitments towards sustainability. While Climate Neutral is still a very young certificate, they are working hard to make themselves known to consumers. They remark, "We believe that the consumer has largely been left out of the picture by other labels and standards, so we're spending a lot of time thinking about how to make our label meaningful, useful, and trusted.[54]"

Awards from independent authorities are an excellent way to earn the trust of consumers. The most common are awards from consumer associations' product tests, like "best buy" or "best product." While independent authorities don't reveal the criteria behind their awards, it is often possible to reverse engineer them and design your product accordingly, increasing your chances of winning such an award. Official institutes also offer another type of awards: safety ratings. Tesla's Model 3, Model S, and Model X have all been given a 5-star safety rating from the National Highway Traffic Safety Administration (NHTSA), a remarkable achievement for such a young brand. In their early years especially, Tesla addressed consumer worries about electric cars' accident safety by prominently featuring the safety rating in their advertising.

Scientific evidence

is one of the most trustworthy forms of endorsement. Scientific evidence is an excellent way to show your product's efficacy and a form of independent third-party endorsement. Companies pursuing this strategy often engage in long-term collaborations with academic institutions, offering them a valuable resource for research and development. For example, Philips has a long history of academic collaboration and backs its product claims with scientific evidence. Scientific evidence is also an important way to substantiate thought leadership, as we saw in the aforementioned Lexilife example.

Design for Ease of Use

Making your product easy to use should be one of your key priorities. Most people are not motivated to invest the time and effort required to learn how to operate a product. Their lack of confidence that they can successfully use the product (their self-efficacy expectations) can prevent them from adopting it. While Design for Ease of Use is related to the design strategy Make It Simple (B3), simplicity is not your key benefit here. Instead, you're trying to remove hurdles for adoption.

The look of a product has a significant influence on people's perception of self-efficacy. If products look technical, they can scare off the general public. People may feel their knowledge and skills are inadequate to successfully operate these products. Apple transformed the boxy look of traditional computers with colors and rounded edges, framing their computers as friendly, easy-to-use devices.

Smart product features can lower the threshold for seemingly difficult-to-use products. When it comes to drones, unskilled operators may fear crashing their drone into a tree or building, or losing track of it all together. Drone manufacturer DJI addressed this by implementing the Return To Home feature. When activated, the drone will automatically fly back to you. Many drones also offer easy to use "follow me" capabilities and crash protection features. They can automatically follow you while filming you from above and remain at a safe distance from any object they encounter.

Tiered levels of difficulty matching the user's level of expertise can make overwhelming tasks seem approachable to first-time users. Redison, a music technology company, offers connected drumsticks and a drumming app called Senstroke. The app offers a Beginner Mode and an Advanced Mode. While the Advanced Mode allows users to configure fully customized drum kits, the Beginner Mode skips the drum kit design. It enables users to immediately start practicing the basics on a relatively simple drum kit configuration.

Smart product features can lower the threshold for seemingly difficult-to-use products

Educate and Support Customers

Educating and supporting customers in all phases of the customer journey will enhance their overall experience, boost customer satisfaction, and increase loyalty.

Onboarding is the tech scene's description of the user familiarization process, in which users rapidly acquaint themselves with a product's interface. Implementing onboarding mechanisms in your product will help people handle your product's learning curve. Slack, the popular teams messaging app, was ranked best in class for its onboarding approach. They use their very own Slackbot to show new users around. It's an interactive approach in which the Slackbot responds to the user's input, making onboarding an engaging, fun, and educational journey.

Always-available educational features and services can help eager-to-learn people get the most from their products, creating loyal, happy users. Apple's "tips app" on their iPhone offers easy access to tips categories like Essentials (must-know features you'll love), Genius picks (favorites from their experts), what's new in your latest iOS update, and more. Their "Today at Apple" program is an online and in-store initiative aimed at educating customers about their products' features. Having discovered cool new features, customers feel excited to use their products and are assured of their value.

Support should be available whenever people need it. Besides setting up your own support desk, creating a community of expert users that share knowledge and offer support can assure new customers that support is always available. Ultimaker, a 3D printer manufacturing company, has leveraged its loyal user base into a community forum. They call it a "Community of 3D Printing Experts." Owners can pose any question they have concerning their 3D printer on the forum. Forums like these are also excellent ways for companies to consolidate feedback about their products, as lead users are often the first to test their product's beta releases.

Lower Thresholds for Purchase

People are often hesitant to make purchases, especially large ones, for fear of financial loss if the product doesn't live up to its promises. A generous, no-questions-asked, free return period can help people overcome their reluctance to buy a new tech product. Lexilight, the lamp for dyslexics described earlier, offers customers

a 100-day trial period with free shipping and a full refund in case of dissatisfaction. If you anticipate marketing your product in a similar fashion, design it with potential returns in mind. For example, by designing your product with refurbishment or remanufacturing in mind, you can remake returned items into new products.

Another option to lower a customer's financial risks is to offer your product as a service. Although the total amount they will spend over the product's lifetime will be higher than when purchasing the product upfront, customers can stop at any time. Offering your product as a service means adopting a new business model and can have considerable implications for your product's design. See page 50 for more information.

Build on Metaphors and Analogies

Consumers often look for clues to understand what a product is or how it works. Both the Conception of New-to-the-World Products chapter at the beginning of this book and the Create Familiarity (R12) design strategy shed light on this clue-seeking behavior. Metaphors and analogies can aid consumer understanding by linking your product to something with which they're familiar.

A metaphor is a figure of speech that directly refers to one thing by mentioning another. You can use metaphors to highlight your product's similarity to another. For example, those unfamiliar with LinkedIn may better understand it when they hear that "LinkedIn is Facebook for business professionals." Of course, this metaphor is only useful if your target audience knows and likes Facebook. Those who don't know Facebook will be even more confused and those who don't like Facebook will extend their dislike to LinkedIn.

An analogy is a comparison that sheds light on a product's benefits and functionality. Knock, a home buying and selling company, is on a mission to "make it as easy to trade in your home as it is to trade in your car."

Metaphors and analogies become more powerful when included in your product design, whether that's in the product's form or shape, the product's interface, or the customer journey.

Integrating product design and marketing strategies from the start of your innovation process can help you better mitigate resistance against your product and the technology it uses

MITIGATING RESISTANCE IS NOT ABOUT PERSUADING CONSUMERS TO ADOPT YOUR PRODUCT; IT IS ABOUT DEVELOPING BETTER PRODUCTS THAT TRIGGER LESS RESISTANCE

THANK

THANK YOU

|

Writing this book was one of the most intellectually inspiring and socially challenging journeys I have ever embarked on.

First and foremost, I would like to thank my husband Mohamed and our kids, Jordan and Ramsey, for their unconditional support. Without their flexibility, becoming an author amid a COVID-19 lockdown would not have been possible.

I want to give special thanks to Anna Filippi. We have been collaborating on this project for more than a year and make a great team. I'm also very grateful for the support and help I received in this book's finalization phase: Karin Nypels, Margriet Larmit, Maarten Zinkstok, and Luke Netjes with the book's contents and Giovanni Beccu with the design. Their help vastly improved the quality of the book.

I want to thank all of my colleagues at the Delft University of Technology, Faculty of Industrial Design Engineering, for being a source of inspiration. A special mention goes to Erik Jan Hultink and Jeroen van Erp; their critical reflection was highly constructive.

Thanks to Monika Sunnanväder and Dorien Franken for always responding to my "urgent questions" regarding graphic design. It's wonderful to have such experts on hand.

Thanks to Eloise King-Smith for inspiring me to write this book and to everyone who provided me with feedback throughout the writing process. Finally, I'd like to thank those whose work inspired me, both academics and innovation professionals.

"A special thanks to you for reading the Tech Innovator's Guide. I hope that it will inspire you to Design Things That Make Sense."

Deborah Nas

REFERENCES

1 Parasuraman, A., & Colby, C. L. (2015). An updated and streamlined technology readiness index: TRI 2.0. Journal of service research, 18(1), 59-74.

2 Rogers, E.M. (1995). Diffusion of Innovations, (4th ed.). New York: Free Press.

3 Pew Research Center. (n.d.). Smartphone ownership in advanced economies higher than in emerging. Retrieved from https://www.pewresearch.org/global/2019/02/05/smartphone-ownership-is-growing-rapidly-around-the-world-but-not-always-equally/pg_global-technology-use-2018_2019-02-05_0-01/

4 Adams, D., Fry, S. (2012). The Salmon of Doubt. Pan Macmillan

5 CB Insights (2019). The Top 20 Reasons Startups Fail. Retrieved from https://www.cbinsights.com/research/startup-failure-post-mortem

6 Desmet, P., & Fokkinga, S. (2020). Beyond Maslow's pyramid: introducing a typology of thirteen fundamental needs for human-centered design. Multimodal Technologies and Interaction, 4(3), 38.

7 Jaakkola, E., & Renko, M. (2007). Critical innovation characteristics influencing acceptability of a new pharmaceutical product format. Journal of Marketing ManagemeWnt, 23, 327–346.

8 Ackermann, C. L., Teichert, T., & Truong, Y. (2018). "So, what is it? And do I like it?" New product categorisation and the formation of consumer implicit attitude. Journal of Marketing Management, 34(9-10), 796-818.

9 Deci, E.L.; Ryan, R.M. The "what" and "why" of goal pursuits: Human needs and the self-determination of behavior. Psychol. Inq. 2000, 11, 227–268.

10 Netflix Newsroom. (2017, August 22). Decoding the Defenders: Netflix Unveils the Gateway Shows That Lead to a Heroic Binge. https://about.netflix.com/en/news/decoding-the-defenders-netflix-unveils-the-gateway-shows-that-lead-to-a-heroic-binge

11 O'Reilly. (2019, May 1). Machine Learning for Personalization - Tony Jebara (Netflix). [Video]. YouTube. https://www.youtube.com/watch?v=TBukLWxiyXs&feature=youtu.be

12 Miller, M. (2019, November 5). Malcolm Gladwell on Bridging the Gap Between Innovation and Adoption. PC. https:// uk.pcmag.com/feature/123411/malcolm-gladwell-on-bridging-the-gap-between-innovation-and-adoption.

13 Tukker, A., & Tischner, U. (Eds.). (2006). New Business for Old Europe: Product-Service Development, Competitiveness and Sustainability (1st ed.). Routledge. https://doi.org/10.4324/9781351280600

14 Wininger, S. (2020, January 24). The Sixth Sense. Lemonade. https://www.lemonade.com/blog/the-sixth-sense/

15 Lemonade. (n.d.). The Lemonade Giveback. Retrieved February 7, 2020, from https://www.lemonade.com/giveback

16 Boyano, A., Espinosa, N., & Villanueva, A. (2020). Rescaling the energy label for washing machines: an opportunity to bring technology development and consumer behaviour closer together. Energy Efficiency, 13(1), 51-67.

17 Electric Vehicle Database. (n.d.). Most efficient electric vehicle. Retrieved February 7, 2020, from https://ev-database.org

18 Goldstein, N. J., Cialdini, R. B., & Griskevicius, V. (2008). A room with a viewpoint: Using social norms to motivate environmental conservation in hotels. Journal of consumer Research, 35(3), 472-482.

19 Tiefenbeck, V., Wörner, A., Schöb, S., Fleisch, E., & Staake, T. (2019). Real-time feedback reduces energy consumption among the broader public without financial incentives. Nature Energy, 4(10), 831-832.

20 Apple (2020, November 24). iPhone Battery and Performance. Apple. https://support.apple.com/en-us/HT208387

21 Lindgaard, G., Fernandes, G., Dudek, C., & Brown, J. (2006). Attention web designers: You have 50 milliseconds to make a good first impression!. Behaviour & information technology, 25(2), 115-126.

22 Kadohisa, M. (2013). Effects of odor on emotion, with implications. Frontiers in systems neuroscience, 7, 66.

23 Lehrner, J., Marwinski, G., Lehr, S., Johren, P., & Deecke, L. (2005). Ambient odors of orange and lavender reduce anxiety and improve mood in a dental office. Physiology & Behavior, 86(1-2), 92-95.

24 Tania Luna and LeeAnn Renninger, 2015, Surprise: Embrace the Unpredictable and Engineer the Unexpected, Penguin Group

25 Popper, B. (2016, August 5). Spotify's Release Radar is a personalized playlist of brand-new music. The Verge. https://www.theverge.com/2016/8/5/12380816/spotify-release-radar-personalized-discovery-curation.

26 Redick, S. (2013, May 10). Surprise Is Still the Most Powerful Marketing Tool. Harvard Business Review. https://hbr.org/2013/05/surprise-is-still-the-most-powerful

27 Seaborn, K., & Fels, D. I. (2015). Gamification in theory and action: A survey. International Journal of human-computer studies, 74, 14-31.

28 Rendever. (2018, July 16). Senior smiles for the first time in months. [Video]. YouTube. https://www.youtube.com/watch?v=wJo6SKAqP6E

29 Freedman, D. (2018, December issue). How to Almost Learn Italian. The Atlantic. https://www.theatlantic.com/magazine/archive/2018/12/language-apps-duolingo/573919/

30 Eliot, C. (2016). The autobiography of Benjamin Franklin. New York: P F Collier & Son Company. http://www.gutenberg.org/files/148/148-h/148-h.htm

31 Fitbit. (n.d.). Who we are. Retrieved December 24, 2020, from https://www.fitbit.com/nz/about.

32 Forbes. (2014, February 4). How Fitbit Survived As A Hardware Startup. https://www.forbes.com/sites/roberthof/2014/02/04/how-fitbit-survived-as-a-hardware-startup/?sh=e04d80e19347

33 Greenpeace, Cook, G., Jardim, E., 2017. Guide to Greener Electronics 2017.

34 Benton, D., Coats, E., Hazell, J., 2015. A Circular Economy for Smart Devices: Opportunities in the US, UK and India. Green Alliance, London.

35 van den Berge, R. B. R., Magnier, L., & Mugge, R. (2020). Too good to go? Consumers' replacement behaviour and potential strategies for stimulating product retention. Current Opinion in Psychology.

    Bakker, C. & Hollander, M. den, Hinte, E. Van & Zijlstra, Y. 2014. Products that last: product design for circular business models. TU Delft Library/Marcel den Hollander IDRC; 01 edition.

36 Smith, c. (2017, April 24). No phone has ever performed worse than the Galaxy S8 in SquareTrade's drop test. BGR. https://bgr.com/2017/04/24/galaxy-s8-drop-test-video-squaretrade/

37 Carbon trust (2020, December 15). Product carbon footprint label. Carbon trust. https://www.carbontrust.com/what-we-do/assurance-and-certification/product-carbon-footprint-label

38 Jacoby, J., & Kaplan, L. B. (1972). The components of perceived risk. ACR special volumes.

39 Joinup. (2021, February 10). OSPO Series: A new strategic center in United Kingdom will step into an OSPO role. Retrieved from

40 Snowden, E. [@Snowden]. (2015, November 2). I use Signal every day. #notesforFBI (Spoiler: they already know). [Tweet].Twitter. https://twitter.com/Snowden/status/661313394906161152

41 Kosinski, M., Stillwell, D., & Graepel, T. (2013). Private traits and attributes are predictable from digital records of human behavior. Proceedings of the national academy of sciences, 110(15), 5802-5805.

42 Statista. (2020, 28 February). Facebook: advertising revenue worldwide 2009-2019. Retrieved from https://www.statista.com/statistics/271258/facebooks-advertising-revenue-worldwide/

43 Obar, J. A., & Oeldorf-Hirsch, A. (2020). The biggest lie on the internet: Ignoring the privacy policies and terms of service policies of social networking services. Information, Communication & Society, 23(1), 128-147.

44 Studio Julia Janssen. (n.d.) 0.0146 seconds | 2019 - ongoing performance. Retrieved from https://www.julia-janssen.nl/00146seconds.html

45 Musk, E. [@elonmusk]. (2019, April 5).It's there for when we start competing with Uber/Lyft & people allow their car to earn money for them as part of the Tesla shared autonomy fleet. In case someone messes up your car, you can check the video. [Tweet] Twitter. https://twitter.com/elonmusk/status/1113977924947009536

46 Tesla_saves_lives. [@SavedTesla]. (2020, June 18) Next software update allows you to activate data sharing of your cabin vehicle camera to help Tesla engineers build new safety features: [Image attached] [Tweet]. Twitter. https://twitter.com/SavedTesla/status/1273513282821914624

47 Richter, F. (2020, October 21). How Long Does Apple Support Older iPhone Models? Statista Infographics. Retrieved from https://www.statista.com/chart/5824/ios-iphone-compatibility/

48 Kim, J. (2019, August 20). Mastercard says the no-number Apple Card comes with "enhanced security" users will never see. CNBC. Retrieved from https://www.cnbc.com/2019/08/20/mastercard-no-number-apple-card-comes-with-enhanced-security.html

49 Hardt Hyperloop. (2020, March 10). Pre-feasibility Study Schiphol - Hyperloop

50 Hekkert, PPM., Snelders, HMJJ., & van Wieringen, PCW. (2003). "Most advanced, yet acceptable": typicality and novelty as joint predictors of aesthetic preference in industrial design. British Journal of Psychology, 94, 111-124.

51 Hekkert, P. (2014). Aesthetic responses to design: A battle of impulses. In T. Smith & P. Tinio (Eds.), The Cambridge handbook of the psychology of aesthetics and the arts (pp. 277-299). Cambridge: Cambridge University Press.

52 Raimond Loewy. (n.d.). Biography. Retrieved from https://www.raymondloewy.com/about/biography/

53 CNET Highlights. (2020, August 5). Check out the Z Fold 2's folding hinge. [Video] YouTube. https://www.youtube.com/watch?v=SuP5gv3dzfI

54 Climate Neutral. FAQ: How is Climate Neutral different from other pledges and labels? Retrieved from https://www.climateneutral.org/faq

IMAGE CREDITS

This book's images are published with the approval of their rights holders under a Creative Commons license or under fair use policy. In all cases, the author and publisher have done their utmost to contact image rights holders for image use approval. If you feel that your copyright has been infringed or that your image has been incorrectly credited, please contact the publisher to request changes in subsequent editions.

p.41 Netflix. Stranger Things artwork Netflix. Netflix Technology Blog. netflixtechblog.com/artwork-personalization-c589f074ad76

p.46 Black Edge Production. Moley Robotics kitchen. Moley Robotics on Medium. moleyrobotics.medium.com/moley-robotic-kitchen-has-launched-the-most-detailed-overview-of-its-innovative-technology-e194b848eac8

p.49 Litter Robot. Litter Robot with cat. Litter Robot press kit. www.litter-robot.com/media.html

p.53 Skin Vision. Woman using SkinVision app. SkinVision press kit. www.skinvision.com/press/

p.54 Cozi. Cozi 2019 Street Background. Cozi press media kit. www.cozi.com/press-media-kit/

p.61 Lemonade Inc. Hand holding a mobile phone with Lemonade app. Lemonade press kit. Lemonade.com

p.62 Lightyear. Lightyear One prototype. Lightyear One press kit. lightyear.one

p.67 Elon Musk. Tweet about Tesla sound functionalities. Twitter. twitter.com/elonmusk/status/1180877114226008064

p.68 SenseGlove. Hand wearing SenseGlove Nova. www.senseglove.com

p.74 Rendever. Senior living resident wearing Rendever VR glasses. www.rendever.com

p.83 Fitbit. Fitbit Sense. Fitbit Sense core carbon graphite render, default screen. investor.fitbit.com/press/press-kit/default.aspx

p.93 Ellen MacArthur Foundation. (February 2019). Circular economy systems diagram. www.ellenmacarthurfoundation.org. https://www.ellenmacarthurfoundation.org Drawing based on Braungart & McDonough, Cradle to Cradle (C2C)

p.95 H_Ko. Businessman hold Nokia 3310 in hand. stock.adobe.com

p.97 Bang & Olufsen. Bang & Olufsen Beosound Shape on wall. www.bang-olufsen.com

p.101 Sammy Bailey/Austockphoto. Grandmother and granddaughter using tablet. stock.adobe.com

p.111 Hövding. Hövding 3 - Airbag for urban cyclists. hovding.com

p.119 Candle. Candle Smart Home devices. www.candlesmarthome.com

p.129 Google. Google Account profile Deborah Nas. [Screenshot by Deborah Nas]. myaccount.google.com

p.131 Google. Seamless Setup badge: works with Hey Google. Google.com

p.135 Signify. Philips Hue Bridge V2 next to a lamp. Signify.com

p.144 Hardt Hyperloop. Hardt Hyperloop, UNtudio and Plomp

p.145 Intuition Robotics. ElliQ robot on a table. elliq.com

p.153 Wmarkusen. A photo of Nest Smart Thermostat in cooling mode, on a clean white wall. stock.adobe.com

p.155 Lexilife. Child using Lexilight lamp. lexilife.com

p.157 Waze. Mobile phones mockups showing Navigation app Waze. Waze.com

p.158 Apple. Apple Watch Nike+. www.apple.com/newsroom/2016/09/apple-nike-launch-apple-watch-nike/

Back flap William Rutten. Deborah Nas portrait photo.

COLOPHON

BIS Publishers

Borneostraat 80-A
1094 CP Amsterdam
The Netherlands
T +31 (0)20 515 02 30
bis@bispublishers.com
www.bispublishers.com

ISBN 978 90 6369 614 6

Copyright © 2021
Deborah Nas and BIS Publishers.

Research and Design by *Anna Filippi*
Copy edited by *Luke Netjes and Kit Brookman*
Graphic design by *Giovanni Beccu*

NOW,

GO INNOVATE!